D1162507

SOCIETY AND SANITY

Society and Sanity

BY

F. J. SHEED

SHEED & WARD

New York—1953

Library of Congress Catalog Number: 53-5198

First Printing, January, 1953
Second Printing, June, 1953

Manufactured in the United States of America

Contents

SOCIETY AND SANITY

1

Sanity Is the Point

OUR TREATMENT of *anything* must depend, in the last resort, on what we think it is: for instance, we treat people one way and cats another, because of our idea of what a man is and what a cat is. All our institutions—family, school, trade union, government, laws, customs, anything you please—grew out of what those who made them thought a man was. If you want to understand them profoundly, you must get at the idea of man that they express. There are periods of human history when it is not immediately and obviously necessary to make this sort of profound enquiry. When institutions are long-established, functioning healthily, serving happiness, the mass of men may very well decide simply to live by them and ask no questions. But when anything goes wrong with an institution —so that we have to decide whether to mend it (and if so, how) or to scrap it (and if so, what to put in its place) — then the question what man is immediately becomes not only practical, but of the first practicality.

This is so for two reasons, one of them vital but in our day widely denied, the other vital and not in any day deniable. The first reason is that all social orders are made for men and must be tested by their aptitude to men. There are those who would smile at this, and for the moment I shall not argue with them, but go on to the second reason, which nobody can deny, that all social orders are made *of* men. People making engines study steel, people making statues study marble, people making social systems should study man, for man is as much the raw material of social systems as steel is of engines, or marble of statues. And whereas we are not all making engines or statues, we are all involved in the making of social systems, from small ones like the family, up to the largest, the State to which we belong.

Our whole life consists in getting along with other human beings. In our personal relations, therefore, the question is, how should men be treated; in the political order, the question is exactly the same. Now you cannot intelligently decide how anything should be treated until you are quite clear what the thing is. You cannot know how men should be treated until you are quite clear what a man is.

That is why the word Sanity is in the title of this book. Sanity means seeing what *is,* living in the reality of things. If a man sees what is not—snakes crawling out of his wall-paper, for instance, or himself as Napoleon—he is not sane. The trouble is that we do not always know when people are seeing what is not or failing to see what is, it can happen less spectacularly than in the instances quoted; but the principle abides, mistaking what is not for what is means that sanity is defective. Wishful thinking, for example, taking one's wishes for reality, is mental defect; so is taking one's fears for reality; so is taking anything but what is for reality. Wishful thinking is the commonest, in Sociology and Politics it is almost universal. It is horribly easy. We concentrate upon the thing we want—a particular arrangement of Society, say—so that it grows larger and larger in our mind; we regard obstacles, naturally, with impatience, get no pleasure out of looking at them, look at them less and less, finally stop seeing them: the obstacles are still there, of course, but they are no longer there for us: only the wish is real. We may still allude to the obstacles, but only to assure our hearers, and reassure ourselves, of the firmness of our hold on reality. Wishful thinkers love the slogans of realism—when you hear a speaker say "Facts, gentlemen, are stubborn things," prepare for a ramble through Utopia.

In every field the test of sanity is *what is;* in the field of human relations, the special test is *what man is.* This is the point at which Sociology must be rooted in reality. If it is not, no amount of accurate investigation and scientific weighing of evidence at subsequent stages will heal the defect at its roots.

(1)

But in the whole of our social life Man is overlooked. Man is taken simply as a word, the label for a particular kind of being (the kind to which we belong ourselves), and nobody stops for any serious consideration of what the word means. We proceed immediately to consider how to make the creature happier without ever asking what the creature is. It should be just the other way round. When some new proposal is made which affects the way men live, our immediate reaction is always to ask, Will it make men happier? But this should be the second question, not the first. The first question should be, Does it fit the nature of man?

The total ignoring of this question runs all through modern life. Education provides an illustration perfect enough to be almost farcical. Throughout most of the Western World, the State is regarded as the normal educator. Schools not conducted by it are regarded as eccentric and in most countries they exist only precariously. This situation, I say, is taken as normal, whereas in fact it is grotesque. There are hundreds of definitions of education. But one may take as a minimum definition, one which would be accepted by practically everybody, that education is to fit men for living. Supposing you were to write to the Education Department of your State something to this effect: "I note that you are in the business of fitting men for living. Would you mind telling me what a man is?" The only possible answer would be that we live in a liberal democracy: every man is entitled to accept any religion or philosophy he pleases, and according to its teaching hold his own view—that man is matter, or spirit, or both, or neither: the State does not decide among them, it is wholly neutral, it does not know what a man is. If you were then to write further and say: "I note that as the State you do not know what a man is. Do you know what living is for?" the answer could only be the same—that it is a matter for each citizen to decide for himself, the State is neutral, the State does not know. I have called this grotesque, and that is to flatter it. To be fitting men for living, not only without knowing what man is or what life is for, but without even thinking the questions relevant, indeed without ever having asked them—it is odd beyond all words. Yet it does not strike people as odd. And the depth of their unawareness of its oddness is the measure of the decay of thinking about fundamentals.

Not only do they not see for themselves that it is odd, they cannot even be shown how odd it is. If one presses the point, they simply change the definition of education. The schools, they say, give their pupils a mass of valuable information, and train them in certain techniques so that they can earn a living, integrate with their fellows, and do the things the State requires of its citizens. But this is merely to take the oddness out of the school system by showing the same oddness firmly rooted in the life of society as a whole.

For what makes information valuable? How can we integrate with our fellows unless they are integrated themselves, and how do we know? And, given the strange things that some States *do* require of their citizens, how do we know that our own State's requirements are not harmful to us as men? None of these questions can be answered till we know what man is. Information is valuable if it helps man to be more fully and richly human: a man is integrated when all the elements of his nature are rightly related to one another and to the goal of life: the State must not require anything of its citizens which, with whatever increase of efficiency or material well-being, will diminish them as men. At every turn not only in education, but in the whole life of Society, the treatment of human beings by one another and of the citizens by the State needs testing by the question, What is man. And it is never asked. The State does not know what man is, and is taking more and more control of man's life.

In Karl Marx you see this ignoring of man in the pure form. The Western democracies do not know, or care, what man is, but they have some notion of what men want and how they are likely to react. Marx had not. Those who agree with him and those who disagree are at one in calling him a sociologist. But he was not a sociologist at all. He was a mathematician. Consider a problem in arithmetic: If one boy can mow a lawn in two hours, how long will it take two boys to mow it? The answer, of course, is one hour—two boys would take half the time that one boy would take. But this is mathematics. In fact, the two boys would start talking, arguing, wrestling: they would get their lawnmowers hopelessly entangled, go off for a swim and never come back. That is sociology. This is the sense in which I say that Marx was a mathematician and not a sociologist. He solved all social problems without reference to the human element. He had only to look at the first man he met to see that the Classless Society would not work with human beings. But he never looked: he had his own theory as to what man is and did not need to look! His most notable follower, Lenin, did at least look: he saw that the Classless Society would not fit man, but he did not let that worry him: "The great socialists in foreseeing the arrival [of the Classless Society] pre-supposed a person not like the present man in the street."* In other words, by that time men will be different. Man, of course, is the sociologist's nightmare. It would be pleasant to be able to dismiss him so cavalierly. But it was left to Bernard Shaw, in this as in so many things, to go the whole way. He, too, saw what Lenin saw and Marx did not. His solution had its own charm: "If the human race will not serve, nature must try another experiment." In other words, the Classless Society is an end in itself: if man is not adequate for it, then nature must find some creature that is. But for us, the problem is to construct social institu-

* *Marx-Engels-Leninism,* p. 182.

tions *for ourselves,* not for some unknown race not yet on the horizon, and *of the material available,* namely, men as they are—which includes their real possibilities of improvement, though the sensible sociologist will not exaggerate the possibilities. This precisely is sanity, a steady refusal to lose contact with what is.

(2)

The ignored question arises every day, in relation to a man's handling of himself and his treatment of other people, in the smallest personal and the largest national issues.

To take a question on which there is difference of opinion, Is divorce or free love right? Swallows do not take one wife for life, alley cats are promiscuous; and the most rigid pietist thinks no worse either of swallows or alley cats. Obviously we are back at the question of what man is. We must settle that, before we can give an intelligent answer to these or any other questions of personal morality. It would be a strange coincidence if the answers were the same whether man is a being akin to the angels, or an animal which has made better use of its opportunities than the other animals, or a mere collection of electrons and protons, a chemical formula, a thing for which a doctor might write a prescription.

Matters like divorce and free love, you might say if you knew very little of the world, are personal and can safely be left to the individual to settle as he pleases. Take some more general question which cannot be written off like that. Is it right to handle men solely for our convenience? We put animals to work for us, thinking only of our needs, wholly ignoring their preferences. Our medical men use animals for their experiments, infecting them with appalling diseases, vivisecting them. Is it wrong to make slaves or laboratory guinea-pigs of men, to vivisect men? "Certainly it is wrong," you reply. "You cannot treat men like animals." Personally I agree that you cannot: but only because, knowing what man is, I know how he differs from the lower animals, and what difference the differences make. Which only means that to answer the question intelligently, you have to settle what a man is. It is not enough to say that men would suffer from being enslaved or infected with disease or sliced up. Animals do not enjoy any of these things. Why should we consider a man's feelings and not a pit pony's or a dog's? Obviously it depends on our view of what man is. You think my examples are fantastic, that it will be sufficient to answer that sort of question when it arises. Who wants to treat men like that? If you can ask that, then you have forgotten about the forced-labour camps of Russia today, the scientific experiments on living men in German concentration camps a few years ago. You may never personally meet a man, although our whole civilization is threatened by a system, that argues in favour of these things. But if you do meet such a man, you will not be able to refute his arguments unless you can state, *and support,* a view of what man is that renders them untenable.

I do not want to go on multiplying examples every one of which will seem more obvious than the one before it. Once we are aware of this line of thought, it is clear that all intelligent sociology is bound up with it. We attach, for example, immense value to human equality. All men, we say, are equal. But equal in what? There is not a single quality in which all men are equal, or in which any two men are equal. Is the phrase meaningless? It has meaning only on one condition, a condition which most of those who use it do not fulfil. All men are equal only in the sense that all men are equally men, just as all triangles are triangles, or all elephants, elephants. So that men are equal to one another in all that is involved in being a man. But we do not know what is involved in being a man, till we know what a man is.

Indeed something even more obviously practical than human equality is at stake, namely human rights. The phrase "rights of man" too often means what it is good, or humane, or socially useful to concede him. But concessions, however liberal, are not rights. Rights are what man is entitled to, not what society is willing to let him have. They belong to man because he is man, and are valid even against society. Unless they are this, they are not rights at all, but only a more or less hopeful expectation of society's kindness. But *has* man rights? Obviously the answer depends on what man is.

I repeat that in quiet times where customs long established go their untroubled way, questions like this might be left to the philosopher. But in our own day there is not a single human institution that is not under fire. Every question under discussion, every revolutionary idea and every conservative reaction—all boil down to the question *how should man be treated,* and we can only answer this in the light of our view of *what man is.* No society can be united, if it is not united about this fundamental question. The United Kingdom is not thus united, nor the United

States, nor the United Nations. The case is not so bad with the first two, because both our nations inherit certain ways of living and acting together, established by ancestors who did agree as to what man is. The United Nations has no such common past. There is neither present agreement in principle as to how man should be treated, nor any agreement in practice flowing out of a long past, for the United Nations has no past, and its constituent members inherit no common attitude to man. But we of the United States or the United Kingdom are in only slightly better case. We will not forever go on agreeing in practical action when all agreement about the reality involved has vanished.

(3)

My personal experience is that it is intensely difficult to persuade anyone to settle down to thought along these lines. The first reaction is usually of the bluff and hearty type—with a quotation, perhaps, of Robert Burns' famous line, "A man's a man for a' that." The dialect does not help. The line tells us that a man is a man. Splendid. But what is a man? When one persists in this way, there is the beginning of irritation. Your interlocutor tells you that everybody knows what a man is, and that it is mere foolishness to waste time on what everybody knows. But in fact everybody does not know, because everybody does not agree: and on this matter the disagreements are so wide that whoever is right, the majority will be wrong.

At this your man will play his trump card, which happens to be his last card. In a desperate effort to avoid the catastrophe of having to think about the question, he will fall back upon that practical working agreement as to how man should be treated which we inherit from our more intelligent ancestors. He will say that we have arrived at a good sound working idea of how people should be treated, and do not need to waste time spinning theories about it. Everyone, he will say—warming to his theme—knows perfectly well the right and wrong way to treat human beings. The trouble is, though we have small hope of getting our man to see it, that what everyone knows, no one knows very thoroughly. Because everyone knows it, we all take it for granted, which means that we do not think about it. There is an absolute deadliness about questions that never get asked because everybody knows the answer—for when they do get asked, no one has an answer ready. We can only get red in the face.

That is precisely what is happening now that we find ourselves up against the Soviet rulers of Russia, who treat men in a way that seems to us intolerable. We are quite incapable of having any reasoned discussion with them on the subject. For that would mean showing them that our way of treating men is right and their way wrong, which can only be done if we show that our view of man is right and theirs wrong. And that we cannot do, because we do not know what our own view of man is. All we can do, in this unhappy circumstance, is to tell the Russians that we personally dislike, and indeed find revolting, their treatment of human beings. They reply that they like it and do not find it revolting. But this is not arguing at all. They state the kind of treatment that they think suitable, we reply with the kind of treatment we like. In other words, we are simply informing them of our prejudice or emotional reaction in the matter. There is no possibility of settling the difference by discussion, since we have not got at the root question without which discussion is impossible. Every phrase we use shows that we have not realized our fundamental inadequacy. I remember being urged to vote for a particular political party because it would get along well with the Russians—"We speak their language." The truth is we do not speak any language. We just feel strongly and splutter. Our lack of clarity about the elementary word, "man," means that none of our subsequent words have any clear meaning.

The Russian rulers, be it noted, are not in this dilemma. They do know what they mean by man. They happen to be wrong, having got their view of man from Marx, who had not looked at man; but they are quite clear about it and they can justify their treatment of man by it. This gives them an enormous advantage in all discussion with the West. No Russian has ever urged as a qualification for office that he speaks *our* language. Indeed, any good Communist would despise himself for making such a claim. For he does speak a language, and our representative men do not. That is why every interchange between ourselves and the Soviet rulers is so humiliating. During the war, for instance, there was the pretence that they and we were partners in a crusade—a pretence which, to do them justice, they hardly bothered to make: they left the lying to us, for they knew we were not partners and could not be—precisely because we do not hold the same views of what man is and cannot therefore hold the same views about how man should be treated. The disparity will continue until we learn to be as clear about our fundamentals as they are about theirs. Then indeed we could really enter into an adult discussion with them. Unless we do, there will ultimately be only one resort. In the impossibility of discussion, we shall only be able to hurl high explosive at each other. Whichever of us has some high explosive left at the end will have won the war: but he will not have won the argument: there will not even have been an argument: an exchange of prejudices is no more an argument than an exchange of high explosive.

So that our practical agreement within our own nations as to how men should be treated—namely, that they should be treated kindly—gets us nowhere when we come up against someone who doesn't agree. How serviceable is it within our own national society? The tendency with us is (1) not to enquire what man is: but (2) not to impose on man anything against which experience has shown that he is likely to react violently: and so to veil from our own eyes the certainly catastrophic results of not making that initial enquiry. Our rule of being as kind to everybody as the circumstances will allow is a well-meaning rule and does us credit, but more credit to our hearts than our heads, for it is a blind rule. The first of the rights of man is not to be treated kindly, but to be treated rightly, to be treated as what he is. Kindness can destroy a man as certainly as cruelty. The French Revolution provides us with a relevant parable. Told that the people had no bread, the king's minister, Foulon, replied, "Let them eat grass," the king's wife, Marie Antoinette, said, "Why don't they eat cake?"* Foulon was cruel and Marie Antoinette was kind. The French Revolution killed them both, and there was a kind of wild

* I know that *"gâteaux"* here probably does not mean cake; and it may not have been Marie Antoinette who said it. But I am using it as a parable, not as a fact.

justice in it, for men will die on a diet of cake just as they will die on a diet of grass. The first question is not of kindness or cruelty, but of rightness or wrongness. Kindness in a doctor treating the human body is no substitute for rightness, nor in anyone else doing anything else, above all not in the social order. The first of the rights of man is to be treated as what he is. What is he?

MAN

2

Man Essential

(1)

OUR CIVILIZATION, the one that used to be called Christian and is now called Western, is based upon the idea our ancestors had of what man is. That idea was clear, strong, universally accepted. They arrived at it, not by looking at man, but by listening to God.

Summarized, it was this:

Man is a creature of God, living in a universe created by God. But he differs from every other being in the world because God made him in His own image.

This special likeness to God is not in man's body, by which he is akin to the animals, but in his soul, which is spiritual, immortal, and meant for eternal union with God.

By setting his will against God's, man had damaged himself and lost oneness with God. God became man and died to save all men from this derelict condition.

In these three ideas—image of God, immortal spirit, redeemed by Christ—you have the dominating elements in that concept of man which went to the building of our civilization.

Now to many this will seem sheerly fantastic, the exhalation of a myth which has curiously managed to survive from a simpler world, or better, has not quite managed to die in a world that has no use for it. And even among those who still regard that view of man as wholly or mainly valid, many would feel that it has no place in a practical discussion of modern problems—that is not the way modern sociologists think. But this, at least, is no argument against it. Considering the appalling mess in which the world is—two blood-baths in a half century and another in horrifying prospect—one cannot approach the way modern sociologists think with any very paralyzing reverence. It could hardly be an argument against *any* theory that it differs from modern thought-processes. But for the moment, I am not urging that earlier view of man as immediately practical or even usable—though I think, and shall try to show later in this book, that it uniquely is both. I merely say that a great civilization was built upon it, that that civilization is now in agony—death throes, maybe, birth throes maybe, but throes beyond a doubt; that to do anything about it, we must understand it, and that there is no understanding it apart from the idea of man it was trying to express. So let us look at it again in a little more detail. No idea has ever been so dynamic, at once so revolutionary and so powerful for constructing a way of life. Even one who does not himself hold it should see that the effort to grasp it *must* be made.

(2)

Take the first phrase—man is made in the image of God. This might mean anything, according to the view of God involved. Man made in the image of the God

Moloch, to whom the Carthaginians sacrificed small children, would have been a horrifying creature, and indeed a sufficient number of men have set out to re-make themselves in that image. But our Christian ancestors knew the truth about God. He is all-powerful, all-knowing, all-loving. Man, made in His image, has all these attributes but limitedly. Man has power, though not all power, knowledge, though not all knowledge, love, though by no means infinite love. God is the absolute, man the image. But the image need not be static. It can deteriorate and be hardly recognizable. But it can grow, too. Men can increase in power, knowledge and love—in other words, in likeness to God. God is in no fear that His creatures may equal Him, the infinite cannot fear the finite: it is altogether according to God's will that the original likeness in all men shall grow greater and greater.

The key to the understanding of God and man is the concept of *spirit*. God is infinite spirit, but one of the elements in man is spirit too, and in this the likeness consists. What is of the essence of spirit—that without which it would not be spirit at all, which must be present therefore, with whatever differences of mode, in infinite spirit and finite—is *permanence*. It is not composed of parts as matter is; so that it cannot fall apart or be taken apart or re-arranged internally. A spiritual being can only be itself, it cannot be made into any other, its norm is immortality. As permanence is the norm of spirit's existence, so is freedom the norm of its vital activity: in its twin functions of knowing and loving, its life consists: for that life, what it *loves* is decisive; and the faculty by which it loves, the will, is free.

Man was made by God for union with Himself. The

finite spirit is to come to a total union with the infinite spirit, in which man's knowing-power will be in immediate, never-to-be-broken contact with infinite truth, and man's loving-power in a contact as close with infinite goodness. And in this contact it will remain itself, not losing its identity in the mightier reality, but conscious of God and conscious of itself as now at last His perfect image.

No one of the religions that concentrate wholly upon spirit to the contempt of matter has ever so glorified man's spirit, for all of them see only extinction, or at any rate the extinction of personal consciousness, as its highest goal. And just as none of the religions of pure spirit glorify spirit as does Christianity, which sees man as spirit united with matter, so none of the philosophies that dismiss spirit and stake their all upon matter so glorify the body. For Christianity the body is sacred, being lifted by the intimacy of its union with the soul out of mere earthiness, and has a place in man's eternal destiny. One can hardly reproach the materialist for not giving the body sacredness, since materialism lacks that concept, knowing only the profane. But he cannot give it things he *can* conceive and indeed long for—conquest of death or any ground of dignity. For the Christian, the body, after the temporary dissolution of death, will be reunited to the soul of man and share his destiny forever. Of all religions, Christianity alone accepts the body fully and ungrudgingly. It brings it into the most sacred places of religion, even to the holy of holies, the Eucharist itself where Christ enters man to be the food of his life and the bond of union among the men that are fed with that food. It is a foundation formula of all Christian Sociology that while spirit is primary, the body has its own sacredness. If either element in that formula is lost, the whole balance is destroyed.

Man, the image of God—by his own nature as spirit and matter binding the two spheres of spirit and matter into one universe, which but for it must ever remain two—lives under law. The material world has its laws given by God, and man's bodily health consists in discovering them and living in accord with them. But the spiritual world equally has laws given by God, and man's spiritual health consists in discovering them and living according to them.

Which brings us to the one element still to consider in the Christian picture of man. The will of man is free, free to accept, but free also to refuse, co-operation—whether with God's will as a whole or with some detail of God's law. Man has, both as a race and each man for himself, partially or totally refused co-operation. He has hurled himself against God's laws and been broken by them. The major breach, resultant from the refusal of man as a race, Christ healed, dying for all men, making that ultimate total union with God possible for all men. But every man must work out his own salvation, and he brings a nature pretty badly knocked about by sin to the task. To the end, the choice is his. He may choose God, or self without God, heaven or hell. Whichever he has chosen at the end of his life upon earth, he has chosen eternally. In other words, man's eternal destiny depends upon his own decision. Responsibility is of man's essence.

(3)

I have said that our ancestors arrived at this view of man not by looking at man but by listening to God. Yet, as it seems to me, a large part of it could have been arrived at, and all of it confirmed, by looking at man: in other words reason can establish the main lines of it, and experience verify all of it.

So let us look at man. This is more depressing than the other way, because God sees the elements of nobility in his creature a great deal more easily than we, with our damaged perspective and our ingrained habit of seeing the nearest as the biggest, possibly can. Similarly, this second way is harder, because man is more likely to overlook elements in himself than is his creator.

Indeed men have never been very good at seeing man aright—and I repeat that I say this not because in a general way men disagree with *my* view, but because they disagree so much among themselves that whoever is right, the majority must be wrong. The people referred to in the first chapter, who think our enquiry not worth making because all men are agreed in practice as to what man is, cannot have travelled widely in the present or read widely of the past. On this particular matter there is simply no point in taking a plebiscite of the human race. Omitting—though a plebiscite would not be entitled to—those who hold (or at any rate say) that nothing at all exists, those others who hold (or say) that nothing exists but themselves, and those who have never thought about the matter and cannot be induced to—we still have vast differences.

There are the three major divisions, those who see man as a union of matter and spirit; those who think that

man is only his body; and those who think that man is, essentially, only his soul. These last can be redivided among those who think that the body is not there at all and our awareness of it only some sort of psychological freak from which man needs to be cured; and those who think that the body is really there but ought not to be, and that the way of development of the personality is to be rid of the body. These latter again are divided by the reasons they advance for man's being afflicted with the unhappy heritage of the body.

The people who admit the soul differ as to whether their will is free or not, and whether the intellect has valid knowledge, and indeed whether the phrase valid knowledge has any meaning, and if so what. The people who deny or disparage the body differ as to the practical consequences of their view: some say that the body should be ignored in the hope that if you don't look at it it will go away, some that it should be maltreated by an extreme asceticism so that it will fall away, some that as the body does not matter it does not matter what we do with it, so that they can plunge into any sort of bodily indulgence with no detriment to their purity.

It would be quite mad to think that men thus divided as to what man is should be capable of a rough working agreement as to how man should be treated. One who holds that such an agreement is possible always means that men universally would be sensible enough to accept the view held in his own particular suburb.

But if men diverge thus widely from one another as to their interpretation of the evidence about man, there is no divergence as to what the evidence is. All men see men doing the same things, suffering the same things,

reacting in the same patterns. But in their interpretation of the evidence, they practically all make the same error—they treat a part, the part that seems most obvious to them, as though it were the whole. All the rest, less obvious, is simply left out. This involves writing off large masses of human experience as delusion, a habit which is in the beginning laziness and in the end paralysis. The materialist explains all the spiritual, to say nothing of the mystical, experience of mankind as delusion; the idealist writes off all the evidence of the senses as delusion. Only the Christian writes off no universal human experience. He accepts the whole of the evidence.

As I have said, as to what the evidence is there is no divergence. However he may explain the fact, everybody sees man with a body, sees that body occupying space, sees the multifarious ways of its relationship with the material universe, including the fact of transience—every material thing holding its own nature insecurely, precariously, always liable to cease to be what it is and to become some other thing. All men see that matter is so and the human body so.

But equally all men, however they may explain the fact, are aware of themselves as thinking. Nor is there any real divergence as to the way our thoughts are experienced by us. The most convinced materialist will admit that an idea has no length or height or breadth or weight or colour or resistance to the touch, or power to be smelled by the nose or tasted by the palate. (An idea may be accompanied by modifications of the brain structure, but these modifications are not the idea itself, as a moment's thought will show.) Nor has it the particular here-and-nowness of matter—a tree can exist only as this

or that individual tree, whereas the idea "tree" can be applied to every tree that ever has been, will be, or could be. But man is continually producing these things, things which in themselves have not one single quality in common with the matter of man's body. It would seem to require an act almost heroic on his part to say that man's body produces things which have no quality in common with it whatever. "The brain secretes thought as the liver secretes bile," says one of these heroes. But bile has so much in common with the parent liver—it occupies space, has weight and dimensions and colour, is that particular bile and not some universal concept of bile. A thought has no quality in common with the brain: I say it is heroic to assert parentage in the face of such total unlikeness.

Looking at the evidence, the Christian accepts it all. The body is there, real, akin to the whole universe of matter. But the body is not the whole story. To account for the totally unbodily elements in man's operation, there is in man's make-up an element as totally unbodily. And man is not either of these elements, nor a chance juxtaposition of them, but an organic compound of them. The Christian looks at this strange union of the bodily and the non-bodily, of spirit and matter, and sees himself as not two beings, but one being, sees his spirit affecting his body and affected by it, sees his body affecting his spirit and responding to it. Further, thinking on about spirit he sees something else. Thought, and therefore that spiritual element in man which is thought's parent, has not one quality in common with man's body. And he sees that the disintegration of the body, which spells death, arises from just those elements in the body which the soul most conspicuously lacks. There is nothing whatever to indicate that the soul does end when the body disintegrates, and reason simply asks how can it possibly end? It does not occupy space, it is not composed of parts, how can it fall apart? If religion says that the soul does not die, it is hard to see how anyone even thinks he can prove religion wrong.

Thus, looking at man with a willingness to accept all the evidence and the refusal to dismiss as illusion such of the evidence as we find difficult to fit in, we see him as a union of matter and spirit, an animal therefore but rational; and we see that spiritual part of him as immortal, with a destiny therefore beyond this life. So that man is a being not contained by the life of this world. He is going, not staying—going somewhere says the Christian, going nowhere says materialism, but by all agreement going: this life is a road, not a home.

It is equally part of the evidence that man is not the cause even of himself, much less of the universe. Man did not make himself, and man did not make the universe in which he finds himself. It is a great simplification at the moment, leading to enormous complications later, to ignore these vast and obvious facts, and start with man and the universe as we find them. But starting in the middle of a story is not the best way to understand it. Whatever is the explanation of man and universe being in existence at all *must* have a profound bearing on what is to happen to them. It was all very well for Marx to say that our business is not to understand the world, but to change it. All experience says that if you try to change something that you don't understand, you will probably destroy it and possibly yourself with it. For one who decides to face this initial question—how anything comes to be here at all—there are only two possible answers: that some mind brought things into being, or that the whole thing is chance. In other words we find at the beginning of all things either God producing or an accident happening.

Behind these two answers men have ranged themselves. The men who made our civilization believed that the universe was created by God. That being so, they assumed that one must take God's views into account! It was not thinkable—by them, or by me, or, one would have thought, by anyone—that if God bothered to make men at all, He did not care what man did with the existence thus given him; it is if anything even less thinkable that what God wishes does not matter. Anyhow what is certain is that the whole structure of civilization known to us was built upon the foundations of belief in the existence of God and the importance of God's will for human action. That foundation has been a good deal eaten away, partly by denial, but mainly by sheer neglect. And no new foundation has been attempted.

I have said that men range themselves behind the one answer or the other: but not in equal proportions. I think it is fair to say that in some form or other the theistic answer is the one that human reason—using the term to mean the actual thinking of the race—has given. And reason—using the term now to mean the mind working by the strictest logic—gives the same answer. A brief survey of man's practically universal reaction will show how reasonable human reason has been in this matter. Looking at the universe, man has been conscious of a vast framework of order. There have been large areas that he did not understand, and elements which he could not see how to fit into the general framework. But these were problems inviting further investigation: whereas the framework was a fact that simply imposed itself, so that it required no hard labour of investigation to establish it. That there is an order, and a magnificent order, man has always seen. Now the human mind revolts at chance as an explanation of even a very simple instance of order—for example, if a man were to see four sticks of equal length lying on the ground at right angles one to another, it would be quite useless to tell him that the wind had blown them there. When Robinson Crusoe saw the sand shaped to a human footprint, he knew that a man had walked there—he did not simply think this a more probable explanation than that the sand had chanced to blow that way, he knew it. Faced with the immeasurably complex order of the universe, man has regarded it as obvious that it must have been produced by a mind and a will.

Indeed, since there is an order in the universe that staggers the mind of man, the obvious explanation would seem to be that it has been caused by a mind immeasurably greater than the mind of a man, a mind of which man's is an image, but the bare image and no more. Anyone who says that an order so massive and multifarious has come about by sheer chance ought surely to feel that the onus of proof for a statement so incredible is on him. But in this matter, as in the matter of the spiritual element in man, the materialist has performed an extraordinary sleight-of-hand trick, and the theist has too often let him get away with it. The materialist, beamingly explaining that this vast interlocking order merely happened that way, has managed to pose as the plain blunt man, cutting away with the knife of his common sense all this nonsense about order being produced by a mind!

When the materialist gets down to a real effort to explain how chance might produce order, he reaches the ultimate in fantasy, yet never loses his air of patient reasonableness. One remembers Huxley's illustration of the monkey with the typewriter: a monkey tapping away through endless ages on a typewriter would ultimately have produced every combination of letters, including that combination of letters which we call *Hamlet*. Similarly, those atoms of which the universe is composed, merely bashing about in limitless space, will ultimately arrange themselves in every possible combination, including that combination which we call our universe. Huxley, as it happens, was not the inventor of this pleasant conceit. The Greeks knew it, without the typewriter of course, in the fifth century before Christ, and prided themselves on having seen through it. The Romans applied it to the poems of Ennius, and thought it frightfully funny. Which of course it is. As between the man who, reading *Hamlet,* assumes it was written by someone and the man who thinks it may be just one of the arrangements of words produced by a monkey with all eternity on his hands, there can hardly be any question which is the plain man and which the fantasist.

Once we come to see, whether along some such line as the one just sketched or by the deeper-thrusting reasonings of the philosophers, that God exists, it is hard to escape the notion of God as having a will for mankind, and giving man some indication of what it is. From this to the notion that God would tell man what ways of action were good for him and what bad is a single step. Taking that step, we arrive at the Moral Law.

At the beginning of this section, I said that reason establishes the major part of the Christian view of man, and confirms all of it. The remainder of this book will be largely concerned with that greater matter of the confirmation of the Christian view of man by reflection upon human experience. It is the literal truth that to one who has really mastered what Christ has to teach about the nature of man, nothing that happens gives any reason for doubt. That view of man is wide enough to take in all human experience.

(4)

We are now in a position to look again at the rights of man. We know now that he *has* rights, real rights not merely concessions, for they are rooted not in Society's notion of the best way to treat its members, but in the nature God gave him. God made him a particular kind of being: He wants him to be treated accordingly, by others and himself. Men, says America's Declaration of Independence, "are endowed by their Creator with certain unalienable rights." And we begin to see what their rights are.

We have seen that the first of the rights of man is to be treated as what he is, and by now we know what he is. He has the right to act as what he is, to move towards the goal for which he has been made: the order of reality is affronted if any one of these rights is denied. He is a union of body and spirit, he has a right to his bodily integrity and the normal development of his bodily powers

—to food therefore and to shelter and to clothing and to healing; he has a right to his spiritual integrity, and the normal development of the powers of his soul. He has a right to life, because his life upon earth is that by which he decides what his eternal destiny is to be. He has a right to be treated according to the Moral Law. He has a right to enter into relation with God, to grow in union with God here with a view to that perfect union which is to come hereafter.

In considering man's rights, there are two further elements. The first of these, the effect upon them of the social order, which is also willed by God and brings with it further rights and a complex of duties, will be discussed later. The second is the effect upon them of sin—a man, handling himself in ways forbidden by the Moral Law, may forfeit his rights. They are not alienable—by anybody but himself: but he can alienate them.

From the Christian view of man, these rights flow. From any other view what rights flow? This is no academic question. *Sociologically it has become for our century the question of questions.* Every man should examine himself most closely upon it.

Take two of the most fundamental of human rights—has the man the right to life, has he the right to liberty? Yes, you say vigorously, even violently: you are certain of both: you are prepared to fight for them. But vigour and violence and certitude and willingness to fight are no proof of truth, they are found as often with error. Has man in fact these two rights? If you meet one who questions either right, how do you show him that man has both? You will find yourself hard pressed to establish them without considering what man is: it would be a highly mystical position to maintain that man has these rights, no matter what he is—that if he is a chemical formula, he has a right to life and liberty; if he is an animal, different only in degree of development from the other animals, he has a right to life and liberty! No other chemical formula has such rights, no other animal.

One remembers Shylock's speech in *The Merchant of Venice:*

> "I am a Jew. Hath not a Jew eyes? Hath not a Jew hands, organs, dimensions, senses, affections, passions? fed with the same food, hurt with the same weapons, subject to the same diseases, healed by the same means, warmed and cooled by the same winter and summer, as a Christian is? If you prick us, do we not bleed? If you tickle us, do we not laugh? If you poison us do we not die?"

It is magnificent, but surprising. One would have expected Shylock to argue that a Jew is a man, even as a Christian is; instead he argues that a Jew is an animal, even as a Christian. If he had been pleading the cause of an ape, instead of his own, he would hardly have needed to alter a word. "Hath not an ape eyes? . . ." What then is the force of the argument? That a Jew has the same human rights as a Christian? Obviously not, for nothing specifically human has been mentioned, and Shylock has far too powerful an intellect to make such an error in logic. He draws from the argument one thing only—"If you wrong us, shall we not revenge?" That is all that could possibly be drawn from it. In man's likeness to the animals is no foundation for human rights.

We use animals to serve our needs—put them to work for us, arrange their mating and their procreating to suit our requirements not theirs, take from them anything they have that we want, kill them for food, or because they are diseased, or because there are too many of them—meaning by that more than we think suitable. Society protects them against wanton ill-treatment, inflicted through callousness or brutality. But to say that animals have *rights* to life and liberty would be farcical. Yet to deny that men have them we should feel to be intolerable. What then is there that man has and animals have not, to serve as foundation for them? It must be some element different in kind, not a mere difference in degree of development, or it will not bear the weight.

The Christian view of man provides such an element. It is hard to see that any other view does. I do not mean that men who reject the Christian view cannot believe passionately in man's rights; often they do, and more effectively than many Christians—for whereas the Christian has sound principles and these others have only sound instincts, the instincts may be alive and operative while the Christian's principles may lie neglected in his mind and fruitless for action. But the men with sound instincts and no more cannot show the rightness of their belief. I have called it mystical, and so it is—a sense of an ultimate mystery in man by which he differs from all other of earth's creatures, man felt more profoundly than he can be formulated. But unformulated, the concept of man's rights cannot be defended against attack—and it is under attack everywhere from those who would treat men, point by point (eating them excepted), as we treat animals. The Christian view gives the formulation, and makes man's rights defensible.

Complaint is often enough made against the Church that she denies or diminishes one or other of man's rights; but only in the view of man that she teaches is there a foundation for any rights at all.

It is to be noted that the rights of man as we have outlined them flow from his being not matter only but spirit as well. Their urgency is intensified by the fact of his immortality—he is responsible for the choices upon which his future without end will depend: anyone who so infringes man's rights as to interfere with the proper use of his powers to bring him to his proper goal is maltreating him and may be damaging him forever.

Note further that one can thus establish man's rights without bringing Christ into the picture. That man is in God's image, free, responsible and immortal, is sufficient foundation for that great structure. Those who see so much must see man as sacred, the eye thus beholding him is aware of vista after vista, leading away beyond its sight into the infinite and eternal. By the time Christianity had begun its march across the world, pagan thought at its highest had come close enough to this concept of man to glimpse his sacredness, and Seneca uttered it in the great phrase—*Homo sacra res homini:* man should be an object of reverence for man. Yet it remains theoretic, not intense enough or urgent enough to produce even in the philosophers a new attitude to man, still less to spread from the philosophers to the multitude and produce a new civilization. It is when we know that God became man and died for men that these other truths come alive, and with power. Many a man who would not be notably moved by philosophical considerations of spirituality and responsibility and likeness to God is shocked into a salutary awareness as he learns of the ultimate proof of God's love for man. In plain fact, Calvary has done what philosophy could never do in bringing into the world a new attitude not only to God who so loved men, but to men who were so loved by God.

3
Reverence

(1)

HOWEVER LITTLE this view of man appeals to you, do not dismiss it lightly. Our first reason for looking at it was that our civilization was built upon it. But there is a better reason still. It is the only view of man upon which a truly human civilization can be built at all; for it is the only view which makes man as such an object of value.

Do not, please, regard this as amiable but academic. We are at the very heart of practicality. Unless man as such is an object of value—every man seen as valuable simply for being a man—then no humanly livable social order is possible. It is not enough to value strong men for being strong, brilliant men for being brilliant, good men for being good. We must value all men for being men, *all* men, weak, stupid, vicious, not only the mediocre average even, but the dismal worst. And we cannot do that unless our view of what man is makes him a thing of value.

"Men must learn to respect one another," said an English politician recently. How true. And how pathetic. In what school are men to learn to respect one another, and by what pedagogy, and what would the lessons be like?

If man is only an animal cleverer than the other animals, with no element in him different in kind, what is there to respect? If man is only a chemical formula, how does one learn to respect electrons, who respects protons? It would be a grim school, in which the teacher would say to the class, "Between you and me, man is not an object of respect: let us learn to respect him. Let us pretend that man is what he is not, and upon that lie shape our social relations." There is no sanity in pretence.

The Christian is not in that degrading dilemma. Christianity taught from the start that every man, *every* man, is made in God's image, has an immortal spirit, and Christ died for him. You are not forced to pretend that such a being is deserving of respect, for he obviously is. This was the most difficult thing that the Church had to persuade men to believe, that every man was of value, simply for being a man. It was difficult, in the first place, because the human race had no habit of it. Even a thinker of Aristotle's quality could relegate slaves to a position not so very different from that of the animals—the farmer, he says, has three sorts of tools, inanimate (ploughs and such), semi-animate (oxen), animate (slaves). Plato criticizes the man who is cruel to slaves—but on the ground that the correct attitude to them is contempt. Plato, indeed, sees no value at all in man simply as man—diseased men should not be kept alive, illegitimate children should be slain in the womb: if they do manage to get themselves born, they must not be allowed to live ("*These are certainly reasonable proposals,* Glaucon said"); and there is something repulsive in his assumption throughout the *Republic* that right treatment for animals is right treatment for men—because, for example, bitches fight like male dogs, women should be sent to war like men.

To the first difficulty, that the human race had no habit of seeing men valuable simply for being men, is added a second—that most people seem to be a denial of the principle. At first view, men do not look so very valuable—there are so many of us, and we are such a mess. Christianity kept steadily hammering at the truth that no matter what a man looked like, he was in the image of God, he had an immortal spirit, Christ had died for him: every man was not only an object of value, but of eternal value. He may have been damaged, deformed almost out of recognition, by his own sins or the injustices of others. But the thing that was damaged was a masterpiece beyond any artist's power to produce: and in face of the masterpiece, mutilated, every instinct of man should cry out for its restoration. It is not tolerable that a masterpiece should remain mutilated if any act of ours can restore it.

This is, I say, the only view of man that makes man an object of respect. Indeed, it makes him an object of reverence. And man must be that or the social order will be inhuman; for men have shown only too clearly that what they do not reverence, they will profane. If they do not reverence man, they will profane man. They will profane other men, they will profane themselves. This is the profanity to which men are almost incurably addicted. You will cure it not by urging them to cease, but by giving them a reason for reverence.

Respect for man is essential to a healthy social order. A sense of human equality is almost as essential. In our own day, most men take for granted that all men are equal, and even the most cynical politician is constrained to give the phrase at least lip service. But we must examine it, to see what it means, or like so much else in our society it will die of neglect. In Chapter 1 the question was raised. Let us look at it again.

Clearly, men are not equal—not all men, not any two men—in any single human attribute. Men are not equally good or equally clever or equally handsome or equally industrious. What then does the phrase mean? Is it purely a legal fiction? Does it mean only that the law will not weight the scales against any man in favour of another man? If it is only a fiction, it will not survive. If we solemnly pretend that men are equal when we know that they are not, a moment will come when the pretence will wear too thin.

The phrase has, of course, a meaning. The trouble is that too often the meaning has no meaning. It means that although men are unequal in all individual human attributes, they are all equally men. I say that this meaning too often has no meaning: for it depends upon what we mean by being a man, which most people do not know or even ask. Is the fact of being a man, in which all men are equal, as important as the attributes in which men are unequal?

Take a rough comparison. One ring might be made of platinum, and another of putty. They are equally circular. But nobody would say that one was as good as the other. The difference between platinum and putty outweighs the similarity of shape. In other words, that by which they are equal is of no great importance. Talk of their equality does not help much. Does the fact of being a man, in which all are alike, outweigh the difference between genius and stupidity, energy and indolence? Only if man matters.

In the Christian view, being a man is itself so vast a thing, that the natural inequalities from one man to the next are a trifle by comparison. In the Christian view, but in no other.

No one, knowing what the words meant, could possibly say, "That man is made in the image of God as I am, but I am richer than he." The phrase would perish in the saying, of its own grotesqueness. It would be the same if a man should say, "That man is an immortal spirit as I am, but I am more learned than he." Or again, "Christ died for that man, as He died for me, but my skin is a more suitable colour." In each of these instances, the similarity admitted is so mighty, the superiority alleged is so trifling in comparison, that a man conscious of what the words mean could not say them, or even think them.

A man could not say any of these things if he knew what he was saying. Yet Christians do in fact say all these things and a score of other things just as silly; and even those of us who would not dream of saying them, act very much as though we believed them. The reason, of course, lies in lack of realization of the mighty realities involved. Most of us give little thought to God or what is meant by being in His image, to spirit or what is meant by its immortality, to redemption or even to Christ who redeemed us. We know these things, but remotely. We may even hold them firmly, so that we would die for them, but not close and clear so that we live by them. Often enough we seem to be betraying them, whereas we have never properly adverted to them. It is hard to conquer the paralysis of habit and routine which make us see what we are used to as though it belonged to the order of nature. The inequalities among men are so very visible: the great spiritual realities that go to the making of every man are hidden, save to the intellect that is prepared to think about them, concentrate its whole gaze on them—till they become not simply ideas known and accepted as true so that it can advert to them when necessary, but part of the very life of the mind, abiding facts of consciousness, things that it literally cannot help being at all times aware of as essential.

That is the ideal, and horribly difficult. Whether we have fully attained it, we can test every time we meet a stranger. If our first reaction is, This is a man, then all is very well. But if our first reaction is, This is a taximan, or a doctor, or a butcher, or a Frenchman, or a Negro, then we are seeing lesser things bigger than greater things. I have spoken of the ideal. Obviously in its fulness it will not be attained by everyone—not by me, I fear. Perhaps only the saint is quite so sane—for sane is the word: since sanity means seeing things as they are, living in the reality of things. And in this reality an immortal spirit redeemed by Christ outweighs all those natural attributes by which here below one such immortal spirit differs from another. If it is too much to expect that every man should realize the truths about man so intensely, at least every man must learn to take them seriously. We must take seriously, if not the more philosophical truths, at least the fact that every man is loved by God and that Our Lord died for all men, so that in making the major decisions of our personal and political lives, we allow them full weight.

Even this is not easy. But no one in his senses would pretend that constructing and maintaining a healthy social order is easy. *"Tantae molis erat Romanam condere gentem*," says Virgil. The founding of the Roman people was so vast a labour. It is a vast labour—and labour that cannot be performed once for all, but must be continually renewed—to make any social order. Thus to see, and keep steadily seeing, the reality by which every man is an object of value is hard, but it will make a healthy society. To throw it aside in favour of some easier sociological formula that will *not* produce a healthy society is folly, the rejection of sanity. Above all, let no one throw it aside without carefully enquiring how, without it, he can answer the same fundamental questions—what is the value of man, and what does human equality mean?

(2)

A very brief survey of man's attitude to man from the smallest things to the biggest will show how far we are, not merely from the ideal reverence already indicated, but from any more than a faint beginning of it. In big things and little, we almost automatically treat men as things, not persons, unless something special in their personality makes us aware that they have a personality. One can start with something as small and daily as our attitude to the waiter in a restaurant. The chances are that we do not so much as look at him, and are not even aware that we have not looked at him unless by chance we want to summon him and then realize that we have not a notion which he is. He is simply a piece of furniture that can take orders. The "thank you" we murmur at the end is a sign rather of good manners than of gratitude, and is usually as mechanically received as given: even in those exceptional cases where there is some faint meaning in the "thank," there is none in the "you": indeed as often as not we omit the "you" altogether and say "thanks." To be able to say the word "you" mechanically is a sign that what should be a vital response in us is now dead.

Examples of the same thing at more serious levels throng on the mind. The special degradation of prostitution, as distinct from an illicit love affair, is that there is no *personal* relationship involved at all. Neither desires the other as that particular person. The man wants relief of physical tension. The woman wants money. Each is a convenience for the other. There is not only no desire for *that* person, there is no desire for any person at all: it is a mere relation of bodily organs. That each wishes it is no more justification for this sort of contract than for a suicide pact—indeed it *is* a kind of suicide pact.

The same thing appears in a different modality in the average relation of employer and employee. It was the special awfulness of the Industrial Revolution that the employer, drawing profit from machines and men, became totally unable to think of either from any other point of view. He found himself having no more personal relation to the men than to the machines. He thought of the men, and talked of them, not as persons but as hands, hands being the only part of them which served him and so held his interest. That the workmen came to regard him with the same impersonality was excusable enough, but none the less tragic. The only issue could be that which has actually come about. Employers and workers now confront each other as two massed forces, aware of each other as persons only when some leader on one side or the other gets himself peculiarly hated—the hatred being of the kind that one does *not* give to machines, but only to persons. It is something that personality should draw even this small tribute, but tragic that it should draw no tribute nobler.

How totally the reverence which ought to be instinctive has vanished one sees again in what I may call our average attitude to machinery, covering under that word not only machines, but processes. The realization never seems to make itself felt that the test of a new method is not whether it will do the work better, but whether it will be better for men that the work should be done that way. We seem incapable of refusing any new invention, or even questioning it. One may take the adding machine as a sort of quick example. Adding machines mean that all the additions are correct, and that everybody has lost the intellectual capacity to add a column of figures. One may agree that it was not any very enormous mental capacity, but capacity it was: it has gone, and it has not been replaced. The small example is not in itself very important. But the principle covers the whole of our society. There is no instinct left in us that leaps to the defence of the assailed human person, no nerve that prompts us even to see the assault.

The examples I have been giving do not in themselves involve any necessary malice or any conscious maltreatment of other human beings. The guest may tip the waiter generously, the hirer has a feeling that his bargain with the prostitute helps her to keep alive, the employer may be a kindly person—one way and another nothing more need be involved than a failure to advert to what ought to be a prime consideration. But man is capable of worse things than that in relation to his fellow-men, involving a direct, conscious, willed misuse of them for his interest, and this is one of the major profanities. To use God's name without reverence is normally a lesser profanity compared with using God's image without reverence: God is more vulnerable in the living man made in His likeness than in the sound by which men have chosen to name Him.

It is part of man's likeness to God that he has intellect by which he can see reality and utter reality as he sees it. To force a man to say what he does not see is the grossest irreverence to man and to God. It blunts man's sense of the value of truth, it twists from its proper use his power of utterance. To prevent a man from saying what he believes is a mild interference, a whole world apart from making him say what he does not believe. It is no service to a doctrine, true or false, to force a man to utter it against his will. You only dishonour the doctrine. When the doctrine is a religious doctrine, it is a way of taking the name of God in vain.

And at that, it is not the worst violation of human personality. To force a man to say what he does not see is gross; but to force a man to *see* what he does not see is the ultimate in profanation. And for that, the modern techniques multiply—"conditioning" is the name for this appalling thing. The human intellect is meant to see in one order of vision, as the eye is meant to see in another. To say to the intellect "See what I tell you" is very much the same as saying it to the eye. But the unhappy difference is that the intellect *can* be thus damaged, whereas the eye cannot. The eye can only be destroyed. But in that case, the man knows he is blind, in the other he thinks he sees. The man seems to survive as a whole man, but he is only part of one. Whether it is the advertiser trying to stun men with slogans, or tyrants weaving the slogans into the very stuff of the life men must live, either way you have man used without reverence. You can destroy a man's "hearing" in that way just as you can by puncturing his ear-drums. Reverence forbids both.

A man is being most simply and responsibly himself when he is doing what he freely chooses in the light of reality as he sees it. He may of course see reality all wrong, and may so act in the light of his wrong vision, or so mis-act even in the light of a right vision, that it may be necessary to check his action and try to correct the defect of intellect or will from which it comes. But any such interference should be approached reluctantly and with reverent fear—as one would approach the restoring of any other damaged masterpiece. The modern social reformer's blithe "I'll rearrange him" is not saved by its essential frivolousness from blasphemy. The work of restoration involves a profound understanding of man's right nature, a profound response to man's essential dignity, a profound awareness of one's own ineffectiveness: it should always be undertaken for the good of the man, or to prevent damage to other men, never to suit one's own self-interest.

(3)

To conclude this chapter, we may apply its principles to two sorts of people whom it has never come easy to men to see justly—people of other races, and people who by defect of mind or body are a burden upon Society.

1. You will find white men looking down upon coloured, civilized men upon savages, Aryans upon Jews, Nordics upon Celts; men of all races tend to see men

of all other races as a lesser kind of men, faintly or markedly grotesque. This pretty universal tendency can be harmless enough; but it can be murderously harmful. Harmful or harmless, it is plain folly.

To arrive at what man is, we simply considered *man:* not white man, civilized man, Aryan man, Nordic man or Australian man (which is the kind of man I am myself). All those adjectives are simply adjectives. No one of them alters the meaning of the word "man." The nature of man and the rights of man are already established before we consider what, if anything, is added by being white, civilized, Aryan, Nordic or Australian. And whatever we have found to be true of the nature of man and the goal of man, and the values and rights of man flowing from the nature and the goal, applies equally to the Negro, the savage, the Jew, and all races and nations whatsoever. Man is a world-wide phenomenon.

The values may or may not be real values which the white man finds in the colour of his skin, the civilized man in the high complexity of his way of life, the Aryan in not being a Jew, everybody in being of his own nationality. But compared with the immeasurable values that go simply with being a man—with being a spiritual creature loved by God, brother to Christ, and with an unbreakable hold upon eternity—these extra small ornaments, even if they have the values their possessors see in them, are almost comically insignificant. Let your white man, civilized man, anti-Semite, citizen of whatever country, be dead three months: and see then how many of his special values remain to distinguish him from the rest of men.

I am not denying that there are differences between men and differences between races. Some men have qualities that others lack, though there are usually, in the apparently less richly endowed, compensating qualities less obvious but equally real; and some races have qualities that others lack, though here again there are usually compensating qualities not realized by the apparently superior race.

But, in the first place, such qualities in the individual are the gift of God, and therefore no reason for pride or conceit in the individual; and such qualities in the race are likewise by God's gift, and in no way due to the individual, who cannot even claim the credit of having chosen or merited to be born into that race. Secondly, we are bound to the same rule of reverence for all men. If we have something that they have not, our whole aim should be to share with them what we have and they haven't—*and* to learn from them what they have and we haven't: anyone who cannot see qualities in another race that his own would be the better for, is simply not very good at looking.

2. That the rights of man are rooted in the nature of man must be kept steadily in mind, as against an already apparent modern tendency to think too much in terms of man's usefulness to Society. Man's claim upon Society lies not in his usefulness to Society, but simply in his being a man. His rights, we have seen, are not simply concessions made to him by Society. Neither are they returns for services rendered to society: he does not earn his right to a livelihood, for example, by social usefulness, though he may lose his claim to it by culpable uselessness. A man may be diseased or crippled or insane: Society still has precisely the same fundamental obligations to him as to its most obviously useful member. Society's obligations

to the individual man are not simply a return for what he does for Society: they arise from the fact that he is a man and that it exists for the good of men. Indeed the quality of a society may be judged by the value it attaches to people who are of the least usefulness to it. Obviously the individual member is bound to serve his fellows according to his capacity: but only according to his capacity. Society is not bound to feed the lazy, but it must feed the helpless. Even then there may be ways of serving Society—for example, by cheerful acceptance of suffering—which would not show in any social balance sheet. But whether or no, man is of value as man: that is the first principle of Christian Sociology.

4
Man Existential

(1)

WHAT WE HAVE BEEN discussing so far is the *essence* of man, true of all men whatsoever, since every man is in fact a union of matter and spirit, made by God, made in God's image, made for God, and redeemed by Christ. When we take one of the Christian definitions of man—man is a union of matter and spirit, for example, or man is a rational animal—we express the essence of humanness, common to all men whatsoever. But to know man, it is not enough to study the definition, we must also keep looking at men. And this for two reasons.

The first is to unfold all the great mass of truth about man wrapped up in the definition. We must study men to find what the definition means; we must study men as they exist, or the essence of man will be only a label. Thus the definition tells us that man is a rational animal: we must look at man to find out how rationality works in an animal, this particular animal. Or to put the same thing in another way, the definition tells us that man knows and loves: and we must study men to find what the knowing process is, what its limits and possibilities are, and what loving means, in a compound of matter and spirit. The definition gives us (to take a handful of examples at random) no information as to the differences between men and women, or as to the part that emotions and passions play in human life, or as to the fascination of money and what man will do for it, or as to the tyranny of the senses—how, for instance, we are slaves to our noses and cannot listen to Socrates if he has bad breath; it gives us not so much as a hint of the whole obscure field of motive.

Indeed, to a mind given to listening to the meanings of words and not only their sounds, the definition itself is a shock. The mind's first reaction must be to cry, Impossible. There are areas of the world where mixed marriages are frowned upon, and courts will dissolve a marriage on the ground of incompatibility. But in all creation there are no two incompatibles so total as spirit and matter. Every man, merely by being a man, is the issue of a mixed marriage. The definition, which merely asserts the marriage, dazzles the mind and gives it precious little light save in fragments and sparkles and half guesses. We must study men to see how the marriage works out—to see what union is possible between these two polar things, to see how the body acts upon the spirit and reacts to it, and how the spirit acts upon the body and reacts to it, to see how at one moment one, at another moment the other, is the dominant partner—for the domination will pass from one to the other in a split second, or hang undecided, to the great misery of the man, for days and months and years. In all the aeons in which men have been studying the union of matter and spirit—which every one of them is—they still have barely got below the surface of this incredible relationship. The mighty things that have flowed from the splitting of the atom are a trifle compared with what flows from even a tiny advance of the human mind into the understanding of the relation of matter and spirit in man. You will not make that advance simply by studying the definition; you will not make it either without studying the definition. What man is and what men are—Man Essential and Man Existential—are two studies, each of which throws a light upon the other without which there would be no real progress in either.

Thus sketchily I have tried to indicate the first reason why it is not enough to study the definition without continuing to study men. The second reason is that while every man verifies the definition, each man verifies it in his own way. Every man is a man; and every man is a different man. The particular sort of man that each man is results from the effect upon the common essence of two facts—that man is damaged, and that man is free. Every one of us inherits something from ancestors, damaged and free; every one of us is environed by fellow-men, damaged and free; every one of us has used himself in such a way as to worsen the damage or correct it, increase the freedom or limit it. It is worth looking for a moment at man as damaged and man as free—remembering that it is not always clear what is due to freedom and what is due to damagedness.

(2)

The Christian believes that owing to a wrong choice made by the common ancestor of the human race, we have all inherited a damaged nature, and that it is one of the effects of the damage that it tends to further damage unless we take powerful action against it. But even one who does not accept the story of that catastrophe at man's origin will not deny that man is a pretty defective being; that, though the degree of defect varies from man to man, none are without it; and that the defect follows certain patterns of damage in man's knowing power and damage in man's operative power.

Let us take a quick look at the damage in man's *knowing* power, more by way of specimens than a methodical investigation. Man is a rational animal. If one knew only the definition and had never met a man, one would assume that a rational animal meant a reasonable animal. In fact we know that man is, just as often, unreasonable. The possession of reason, which distinguishes him from the lower animals, means that he can act reasonably as they cannot, but also unreasonably, as they cannot. The animals, not having reason, cannot misuse it. Man has it, can misuse it, does misuse it. Misusing it, he falls, not to the animal level, but below it. If animals really understood their masters, they would for a great part of the time be unutterably shocked. Man is endlessly ingenious in discovering ways of misusing his reason. The commonest way, perhaps, is to leave it unused. Most of us would rather not think at all when any effort is involved. The use of the body is easy, and promises pleasure. The use of the mind is difficult and holds out no such promises. So man is always trying to by-pass the use of the mind. He thinks with reluctance, which makes him a slave to habit. He thinks with the will, which makes him a slave to desire. He thinks with the imagination, which makes him a slave to slogans. Not using the full power of his mind, he loses perspective. Things closest—that is, closest to the body's power to respond to them—loom biggest. A dead rat in the wainscot afflicts his nose more than a dead whale in the Pacific, so he thinks it smells worse. A shrub close at hand looks larger than Vesuvius on the horizon. One result of all these ingenious ways of avoiding the use of the mind is that man is intensely gullible: offer him happiness, and all his defences are down. And the trouble is that man is not consistent: you cannot even rely upon him to act unreasonably: for he is damaged, but not wholly; and he is free.

Let us take a similar quick look at the defects in man's *operative* power—I do not here mean his power to execute his designs, but that in him by which he chooses, decides, initiates. What we have been looking at so far is man's unreasonability in the sense that he does not reason efficiently. Now we come to unreasonability in the profounder sense, when a man does not act according to what his reason *has* managed to tell him. The line of St. Paul (Rom. vii. 19)—"It is not the good my will prefers but the evil my will disapproves, that I find myself doing"—is true universally. We have all had the experience of seeing what we ought to do, agreeing that we ought to do it, and doing the opposite; and this not only with things which we saw to be abstractly more desirable, or useful for the good of others, but things which sheer self-interest should have made us pursue. Every kind of thing intervenes to prevent us doing the thing we know we ought, in our own interests, to do. There is sloth, for instance, clutching at present ease in the certainty of vastly increased labour tomorrow; there is the power of habits, some of which seem to be beyond our power to uproot; there are passions—anger, for instance, which gives us every day the spectacle of someone (ourself as likely as not) cutting off his nose to spite his face. And over and above all these recognizable causes of unreasonable action, there is the shapeless, nameless, horribly powerful, unpredictable thing which for want of a better name we call cussedness—an irresistible impulse to do the unreasonable thing *because* it is unreasonable. There is in us a diseased craving for the irrational, a hunger and thirst for it.

All this is recognizable, and recognizable as defect, whatever ultimate views of the nature of man or the meaning of life one may have. In the same way it is evident that man is always waging two warfares, war within himself and external war. Within himself there is the clamour of the body and the power of imagination striving against clear vision, right choice; and even when man has dropped every standard save the satisfaction of his lower appetites, he finds that these are forever getting in each other's way, setting themselves incompatible aims, so that to gratify one he must sacrifice another—as when a man wants both alcohol and success in business, or, being a rising politician, needs the help of some political boss while lusting for his wife.

And this same self, torn with civil war, is the greatest single cause of evil in the world, as it quests, clamours, thrusts against other men and against God. But, once more, not consistently: the worst of us do from time to time act well—or at any rate, look as if we easily might.

(3)

For man is free. The wandering mind can concentrate, the tired will can make a stand, the thrusting self is capable of supreme sacrifice. You never know when. There is that element in man which makes him incalculable, even to himself. His will is made to love goodness, as his eye is made to see colour. There is no end to the variety of colours his eye can see, or to the variety of goodnesses his will can love and attach itself to. Provided a thing is seen as good in some way or other the will can set itself upon it: and then may leave it for some other thing seen as good: or not leave it, but try to cling to it and have the other, incompatible, good as well. With the will thus confused by desires pushing out in every direction, the only possible principle of unity is the Supreme Good, seen as such. But here below, even when we see God as the Supreme Good and God's will as the one sane rule of action, we can still be distracted in act and desire to lesser things, because in our curious perspective they can loom larger: even then the awareness of the Supreme Good does not lose its value, since in it we have a standard of judgment, a point of return.

None of this is academic. It is the error of most planners that they build everything on the similarity of men and assume that the differences will make no difference—anyhow they leave no room for them. But room must be left for them. The freedom of man's will does not mean that there are no general tendencies but only individual choices. Men by will are free to choose anything that strikes them as good; but men by nature tend to find the same sorts of thing good. On a given matter, nine men out of ten will tend to make the same choice—but there is always a tenth man: just as a given man will choose the same way nine times out of ten—but there is a tenth time, when he does not. And these exceptional people and exceptional occasions may be of the utmost value, not less so because one cannot calculate their incidence.

If we are to build a social order for beings with this strong element of incalculability, we must be aware of it and leave a margin for it—not a calculable margin naturally, but as much margin as we can possibly manage. One way or another men are trying for happiness—Pope Pius XI, indeed, says that the desire for happiness even here below is in our nature, implanted there by God. Any social order must give at least some minimum satisfaction (though it should be aiming at much more than that) to this desire. But human incalculability is at its most maddening precisely here. Men are, on the plain evidence, hopelessly bad at knowing what will make them happy: and when, almost it would seem by fluke, they find something that does, they can almost never stay happy in it. The mobile will has moved on. We have already seen that ultimate unreasonableness in man which makes him choose the unreasonable for its very unreasonability. You see it very strongly in this matter of happiness possessed. At our best moments there is a sort of malaise, as though every joy which seems most substantial were shot through with fragility and held precariously so that a puff of wind or a whisper can unlock our firmest grip. How far is this a defect in man, unable to hold on to joy? How far is it a defect in things, unable to satisfy long?

In this matter, as so often, the essence of man helps to an understanding of a peculiarity in men. It is, once again, a matter of plain evidence that man's happiness is embedded in personal relations. Persons are far more powerful than things as causes of happiness, precisely because persons are images of God, and things merely bear the traces of God's workmanship. And persons are a cause of a richer and more abiding happiness in proportion as we see them *as* persons and not simply as things. Happiness in a personal relation *can* abide, if we love the image of God in the person, and love the person and God together.

(4)

We must study the bewildering variety of man, but not be bewildered by it. In other words we must keep reverting from men to man, seeing Everyman in each man, seeing each man as one particular way of being Everyman.

What is vital, if we are to play an intelligent part in building any social order at all—family or state, club, school, trade union, anything—is that we study man, not of course as a psychiatrist studies his mind or a doctor his body, but sufficiently to know what man is and what men are like. Some of the reasons for this are so obvious and concrete that one can write them down in a list. But the profoundest reasons escape listing. In any sort of making, the value of intimacy with one's material is greater than can be set down in black and white. And intimacy does not mean knowing one's material so well that one can take it for granted and shape it to one's ends without ever giving it a thought. Intimacy involves love. A sculptor loves stone, and loves it for being stone, loves it for its very resistance to his will, its un-cooperativeness, and not only for his work on it. In the same way a sociologist will be a good sociologist only if he loves man. And I do not mean simply that he should love man spiritually for the highest in him, but the whole tragic-comic complexus of humanity. He must be as far as possible from Bernard Shaw's desire to "abolish the British working class and replace them by sensible people." The man who would build a really good social order should be closer to the ideal seen as unattainable by the amiable critic:

> I wish I loved the human race
> I wish I loved its silly face.

There are dangers in that, too, but profoundly right substance. Anyhow, in so far as we, personally, have to do with the building of healthy families or a healthy Society, we must continue to grow in intimacy with man. We must value the common essence of man because all oneness and brotherhood are in it. We must value the differences from man to man because freedom and richness of growth are in them.

5

Realism

(1)

THE ATTENTIVE READER may note that whereas the chapter on what man essentially is was followed by a chapter on Reverence, the chapter on what men are actually like is followed by one on Realism. The chapter headings do not mean that we are now going to throw a little cold realism on the overheated stuff about reverence, or that, now that we have to be realistic, the original talk about reverence may take some of the chill off our realism. Realism does not exclude reverence, but is in fact demanded by it—it is no reverence to man to say I dare not face the truth about him. But equally it is not realism to omit the elements in man that call for reverence.

It is worth our while to pause for a moment to look at the curious thing that has happened to the word realism. Obviously it should mean taking things as they actually are, taking account of all the facts. As the word is normally used it means being extremely selective about the facts—taking the facts one thinks one can handle. For instance the "realist" about man leaves out of account the facts—which he can hardly fail to know—that man did not make himself, that man will one day die, that he will be a long time dead. One gets the impression that these facts are too big, and that what the realist really likes is a whole mass of little facts, especially the ones that lie immediately under his nose. But even this does not get at the very nerve of his thinking. The facts he really likes to handle, the handling of which distinguishes him as a realist from the sentimental mass of his fellows, are the discreditable facts. And he is immensely pleased with himself for seeing them and scornful of you and me for our blindness to them.

He will tell you—assuming that the fact will certainly have escaped your notice—that the Venus de Milo's arms are broken. He has observed this, with his trained realist's eye. He has indeed. He has scarcely observed anything else about the Venus de Milo. His method closes off the best things from his gaze, but it closes off the worst too. He sees only the surface of evil. The worst horror in evil is the nobility that has been degraded—in the sinner as well as in the victim; but to our realist there *is* no nobility: nothing being sacred, nothing is desecrated. He has no real sense of smell, so that to the Christian he seems spinsterish, full of the small talk of human ignominy but totally unaware of the real horror of life: spinsterish, too, in this other sense that he has never surrendered himself to reality, but has preferred his keyhole to reality's intimate embrace. He calls himself hard-boiled. But no egg ever boasted of being hard-boiled—no sensible egg would get itself boiled at all. A hard-boiled egg will never become a bird: there is no future for that egg, no posterity: the living element has been boiled out of it. Our realist's metaphor has gone astray and got all its values crossed, which is precisely what he has done himself.

You will find the realist in the naked state, so to speak, among the practical politicians. For these men (the Machiavelli who wrote *The Prince* is their arch-priest) the only problem is how should man be handled–that is, bullied, coaxed, bluffed or tricked into doing what they want him to do. Their art, such as it is, lies not in understanding men, but in knowing how men will react. It is the art of getting men to jump through this or that hoop—not the true object of politics, which is to help men to be more completely men. Where the doctor studies man in order to heal him, this sort of blackguard studies man in order to use him. You could make a sort of Politician's Handbook of their rules. *Every man has his price. There's a fool born every minute. Throw enough mud and some of it will stick. If you can't beat them, join them. Today's paper lights tomorrow's fire.* The effect is always to dehumanize, to treat men as being nothing more than the sum of their defects. The lucky politician gets by. His successors reap the miserable harvest. Indeed, in this field, success lies not in solving problems but in postponing them. And the art of it is to treat men as things, which, as we have seen, is profanity.

I have mentioned Machiavelli and his book. When people use realism in the sense I find so odd, it is always of him that they think. He is *the* realist.* He can point certain morals for us.

He wrote *The Prince* and dedicated it to Lorenzo de Medici, ruler of Florence, in the hope that Lorenzo would give him a job, he being then out of one, and destined

* But is he spinsterish? Here is Max Lerner's description of him, from the Introduction to the Modern Library edition of *The Prince:* "A thin-faced, pale little man, with a sharp nose . . . subtle lips . . . a discreet and enigmatic smile . . . eyes that look as if they knew much more than they are willing to tell."

never to have the high post he craved. Its theme is how to win a kingdom in Italy and hang on to it, nothing else: no advice on how to be a good ruler or how to serve the interests of his people: simply how to get power and keep it. It is not a book on politics, therefore, but a sort of Gangster's Manual. As such it has to be tough. "A prince should have no other aim or thought but war." "A prudent ruler ought not to keep faith, when it is against his interest." "A prince must often act against faith, against charity, against humanity, against religion." "Men will always be false to you unless they are compelled by necessity to be true." "Men must either be caressed or annihilated." "A conqueror should commit all his cruelties at once" (it unsettles everybody if he has to keep recurring to them). Caesar Borgia is the ideal prince, and we get a full-length study: including, for example, how he first used a brute called Remirro de Orco to terrorize his subjects into obedience, then in order to purge himself of the hatred thus caused, he had Remirro sawn in half and the bisected body exposed in the public square at Cesena. Machiavelli sums up his study of Caesar—"Reviewing all the actions of the Duke, I find nothing to blame."

One feels, as one reads, that *The Prince* is a marvellously successful piece of irony: in the smiling guise of advice to despots, it is a murderous attack upon despotism, pleading the case for republican government by showing the crimes inseparable from princedom: when, in his larger work, *The Discourses,* he writes of the republic, there is none of this Ruthless-Rhymes-for-Heartless-Homes sort of bloodiness. But no one seems to have taken *The Prince* as irony, and from our present point of view it does not matter; for we are not studying Machiavelli, we are concerned with realism; and taking his book at its face value, men ever since have seen it as realism's very essence.

Max Lerner (in the brilliantly written introduction to *The Prince* cited on page sixty-four, footnote) writes what may be taken as the general view: "The humanists who had written books about princes had written in the idealistic and scholastic medieval tradition; they were ridden by theology and metaphysics. Machiavelli rejected metaphysics, theology, idealism. The whole drift of his work is towards a political realism, unknown to the formal writing of his time." Surely the thing is much simpler. The other humanists of his own day and the medieval thinkers before them were writing on politics, Machiavelli was writing practical advice for tyrants. The other writers knew that such men existed, for history and their own time swarmed with them, and that they used such means; but it did not occur to them to write manuals for their guidance. Had they done so, they would have been as sparing as Machiavelli of theology and metaphysics. "*The Prince,*" Mr. Lerner says further, "places itself squarely in the ranks of realism. It brushes aside, with an impatience in which Machiavelli scarcely cares to conceal his disdain, the tender-mindedness of reformers and idealists." One recognizes that disdainful impatience—Al Capone, one feels, would have brushed aside an appeal to decency precisely thus.

But how realistic is the book? If realistic simply means tough, it is very realistic indeed. But it doesn't. It means seeing the reality of things clearly; and the book omits too much of reality for that. The things theology and metaphysics deal with are, as we have seen, realities, ignoring them the book's guidance is reduced to rule of thumb.

Even the patch of life it does think worthy of attention it misreads—thus "men in general are ungrateful, dissemblers, anxious to avoid danger and covetous of gain": but what else could men be under such a prince, how else could they survive?—his generalization is not true of men in themselves but only of men subjected to his ideal ruler. And by its one supreme test—of practical success—it is most unrealistic of all. Machiavelli, the master himself, was a total failure (indeed, if to cynicism he had added common sense, he would never have let the book get about—for who would dare to employ in any post of high responsibility a man so cunning and unscrupulous as he shows himself in it?). Machiavelli failed. His model prince Caesar Borgia had failed. And most of his best pupils have failed, spectacularly—Napoleon, for instance, had studied him assiduously, so had Mussolini and Hitler.

It may seem strange, in a book as short as my own, to give so much space to *The Prince*. But realism, in its sense, is the greatest present obstacle to healthy relations among men and peoples. I still think it extraordinary that the word realism should be applied to a way of looking at reality that omits so much. Realism means, and must be seen to mean, taking all the facts into account—the essence of man, by which man is an object of reverence; the variety of man, by which man is himself; the defectiveness of man, by which man is an object of compassion.

(2)

Concentrating on Man Existential, to the ignoring of Man Essential, need not mean the kind of baseness I have been describing. Men fail to advert to the essential nature of man either because they do not know it, or because it has never occurred to them that it is relevant to the practical running of life. What is more surprising, indeed immeasurably surprising, is the grimy list of the errors men make through failure even to look at the human race as it lives its life on earth under their very noses. That rulers should ignore man's essence is comprehensible, though not less tragic for that: that they should make and continue to make the grossest errors as to Man Existential is beyond all understanding. There is no limit to the examples.

The men who planned the medieval Inquisition, for example, were serious men, who meant not only well but very well. They burnt heretics, not from hatred of the heretics, but from love of all the souls they saw threatened by heresy. The one result of their action that they did not foresee was the one result which it seems incredible that they should have missed: they caused the Church to be loathed. I am not saying their actions deserved loathing, but only that they were absolutely certain to get it. And they have got it. Had they adverted to this certainty and decided that the necessities of the immediate situation left them no choice, it would have been understandable. My point is that they never adverted to it. Nor did they advert to the possibility that bloodshed might strengthen the heresy. They knew, as an existential fact, that the blood of martyrs was the seed of the Church: it is curious that they had not realized that the blood of martyrs may very well be the seed of practically any institution that has the good fortune to have martyrs. The Church of England, every schoolboy will tell you, was established by Queen Elizabeth. But every schoolboy is wrong. The Church of

England was established by Queen Mary—the people burned by her at Smithfield gave a sacredness to Protestantism and aroused a hatred of Catholicism which neither has wholly lived down in the four centuries since.

Karl Marx did not make the error of thinking that what man is does not matter: he merely made an error as to what man is. We shall return to this. What I am concerned with here is that he not only did not know what man is, he did not even know what man is like. He observed that great evils arise from the ill distribution of property. His solution was simple: abolish property. There is a haunting resemblance here to what America did in 1918. It was observed that great evils arose from the overconsumption of alcohol. The solution was brusque enough to please Marx: abolish alcohol. The two things are classic examples of a failure to look at men. It must be for anthropologists to argue whether alcohol or property is the older human institution. But men have been going in for both for so long that they have become habits. For the intelligent realist, the question of whether they are good habits or bad habits does not mask the fact that they are inveterate habits, and as such cannot just be plucked up out of the soil of man's nature.

All of these and a dozen other things that throng on the mind are examples of gross failures in psychology at its most obvious, and even men who are not interested in the essence of man should not be guilty of them.

Indeed really able students of Man Existential will achieve enormous immediate success in handling men, without ever adverting to Man Essential. Their success can only be temporary. In the long run they themselves and the society they handle will suffer. For in themselves there is no ultimate reason for reverencing man: with whatever ideals they begin, the power to "manage" people, even for their own good, almost always leads to a sort of weary contempt for them, and a sense of one's own superiority to them. Even if the leader is handling them for their own good, he is not handling them according to their human liberty. It is bad for him, as I have just said. That it is bad for them I shall try to show.

(3)

From a neglect of the essential nature of man by those who have to handle the social order, two main streams of consequence flow. In the first place there will be social action which, in varying degrees of error, treats man as what he is not. And in the second place when it becomes unavoidably clear that society, in the persons who constitute it, is sick and must be healed, there is no right notion of human wholeness guiding the efforts of the reformers, so that they are forced to go on experimenting more or less in the dark. Both of these are worth a quick glance here.

Consider one or two ways of treating man as what he is not. Man is a union of matter and spirit, with the power to see reality and to plan his own activities in relation to the reality thus seen. A major dignity of man is that he is responsible; indeed his eternal future depends upon the use he makes of his responsibility. Time and again in the history of mankind social orders are to be found which ignore the spiritual element in man and concentrate upon his material well-being, or ignore the responsibility of man and make more and more decisions for him. For almost any misuse of man, there are two successive reactions. Men begin by rebelling, but usually pass from rebellion to a dulled acquiescence. The misusing of man is always an evil, but it does most harm at the second stage, when men have settled down to it, do not feel oppressed by it, take it so completely for granted that they do not know that they are taking it for granted. At this stage the misuse no longer torments, but devitalizes all the more. Treating any being as what it is not makes it still less completely itself. But vitality is altogether bound up with a thing's being completely itself. Whatever the motive, if a being is diminished, its vitality will be diminished. If you treat men as non-responsible, you make them incapable of initiative, and one source of vitality in them is dried up. If you treat men as though they were bodies only, the spirit is not fed, and undernourishment and devitalization proceed hand in hand. You have what is almost a classroom specimen of all this in the early Roman Empire. The rulers saw, and saw with increasing alarm, that people were ceasing to have children. They met the situation with one of the most futile gestures anywhere recorded. They passed a law giving some extra social and political privileges to fathers of three children. The law was of no effect, naturally. The failure to have children is a failure of vitality, physical or psychological: and the notion that a handful of privileges will restore vitality is clearly pathetic. It was a failure of vitality, an implicit statement that people had lost confidence in life and no longer thought that life was worth bringing children into. And indeed life as it had come to be lived was a sort of twilight life, as a result of that double mutilation of the human person we have just been considering.

Look now at a different way of using man as what he

is not—treating him as though he were an autonomous being and not, as he is, a creature of God, made by God, made for God. We have already looked at the error Karl Marx made about Man Existential in the matter of property. He made a profounder error about Man Essential in the matter of religion: that too was to be abolished. I have called this an error about Man Essential, but indeed it is as gross an error about Man Existential, and that in certain most obvious ways. A French cynic who said that if God did not exist it would be necessary to invent him was, as far as he went, a shrewd observer of human nature—he had at least observed that men lose a principal motive for right conduct when they lose belief in God: and Marx might at least have observed as much. But, at a deeper level, there is recurrence of his error about property.

Property, we remind ourselves, is a very ancient human habit. Religion is a human habit even more ancient. The notion that one can just pluck out something so intimately woven into man's nature is great foolishness. Marx never discovered this, because he never had to make his system work. It existed only on paper, and paper will tolerate anything. Stalin, who was a Marxian as a young man and still, one feels, has a sort of nostalgic affection for the god of his boyhood, did make an effort to make the Marxist system work, in this matter of religion as in other matters. But he was not prepared out of devotion to Marx to tear Russia in pieces, and he finally compromised. He discovered by experience, what the smallest reading of history might have shown him, that you can no more abolish religion by closing the churches than you can abolish sex by making marriage illegal. In this particular instance, the reaction of men to being treated as un-men did not, for

Russians as a whole, need to go beyond the first stage. They resisted, the religious need in them simply went looking for strange outlets when the normal outlet was closed. But when the denial of God goes on long enough to produce the second reaction, acquiescence, then we are able to see that the need for God is not simply something that has grown habitual through the routine of ages so that it belongs solidly to Man Existential; when the habit is apparently and even painlessly broken, we see results which show the profounder truth—that to be made by God and for God is of the essence of man.

Because man was made for God, God has built man with certain powers by which he is to take hold of God, and certain needs by which he is moved to the exercise of these powers. Thus the power to adore, and the need to adore, are as truly in the human make-up as the power and the need man has to nourish himself by food—as truly and much more deeply. They are simply facts. Just as the infant, who has never heard of food, has the power to absorb food, and the need for food, and will certainly perish without it; so every man has the power to adore and the need to adore and will certainly perish if the need is not met. When you have a need as profound as this, and a power as great, they are bound to seek an object. Not knowing God, who is the true Object of their power to adore, men will seek a pseudo-object. With that curious freedom man has, there is no limit to the objects of which he may make substitute gods. But in our own age, two are sensationally in evidence. They have special relevance to the theme of this book, for one is a major cause of disaster in the sexual order, and the other in the political.

A man and a woman, falling in love and knowing nothing of God, almost inevitably make each other the object of that power to adore which is in them as human beings and which for want of its true object works upon them tormentingly. Each adores the other. Each expects of the other what in fact only God can give—a total satisfaction of every deepest need. Naturally, neither gets what he wants: how can either give everything to the other, when neither possesses everything, but needs great floods of divine energy constantly renewed in him by God? Then the tendency is to feel resentful, as though a promise had been made and not kept; and the resentment grows, as each comes to the end of the other's resources, and the emptiness of each becomes for the other a grimmer nightmare with every day that passes.

In the political order we see the need for an absolute upon which man may set his need to adore, in the monstrous totalitarianisms of our time. One significant difference by which the false absolute can always be known as false lies in this—that the State, or Party, or Proletariat, or whatever it may be, demands the total surrender of personality, whereas the true Absolute insists that man be himself: that is the way God wants him to be: if He had not, He would not have made him so. God loves personality. Even in the life of the Trinity, the self of each Person is not merged and dissolved, each remains wholly Himself; and in the closest relation to God so must we.

(4)

Comparing Man Existential with Man Essential does not mean comparing man as he is with man as he ought to be. It is not comparing a fact with an ideal. It is comparing a fact with a fact. Man Essential tells you the fact about man *as man*. Man Existential tells you the fact about man *as this or that individual*. Neither is more factual than the other, neither is more real.

It is essential for man's well-being that the two sets of facts should be in harmony. Comparing Man Existential with Man Essential, we can distinguish between those elements in men which are harmonious with man's nature and those which are in contradiction with it—these last, whatever sense of freedom and enlargement they give, actually make man less man.

Man, as we have seen, is being himself when he is making his own decisions in the light of reality as he sees it. But man is defective all the same. He does not see reality wholly aright, and, when he does, he does not always make his decisions in the light of it. Primarily it is for the man himself to work for the correction of his defects: on occasion it may be necessary for others to do the same—as when the faults of men are the cause of grave injustice to other men, or the common good suffers beyond a point.

Whether we are working upon our own defects or other people's, it is vital that we know the essence of man. Our object must not be to alter man in whatever way strikes us as pleasing but to restore man to the integrity of his own nature—as a doctor dealing with pneumonia tries to heal the affected lung, not to give the patient a third lung. With the body it is easier because there is a fair amount of agreement as to what the integrity of a body is. What the moral, psychological, spiritual norm may be is not so easily known—but just as essential. Not knowing man's true nature, the reformer (of himself or other individuals or society as a whole) must do one of two things. Either he will deal with such symptoms as seem to him especially distressing so that they will stop plaguing the man himself or other men or the community. Or, if he sees the need of a more general plan, he will almost certainly try to remake man in some image—his own best self, probably—that seems to him desirable: Plato's ideal Republic, as someone has remarked, is a state-organized imitation of Socrates, and it is hard not to think that Plato had already remade Socrates in his own image before writing the book. We have already seen the frivolousness of the "I'll rearrange him" type of reformer. There must be the realism which sees that knowledge of the nature to which one seeks to restore man is necessary: and the reverence which feels that there could be no higher aim than to restore man's nature to its own proper excellence.

So we are back at reverence: which must be seen as vitalizing, not paralyzing. We are not meant to be rigid with reverence, but alive with it. Reverence does not mean that we cannot see man's comicality and smile at it, or see man's weaknesses and do something about them—reverence for a sick child may demand that we give it castor oil, a gift not usually thought of in terms of reverence; reverence for a poet would demand that we tell him when we think his poems bad, to praise them would be to treat *him* irreverently. Reverence does not mean shilly-shallying and impotent tiptoeing around for fear of doing damage. What it should be you see in a surgeon operating: for him reverence means the most careful appraisal of the situation—whether an operation is needed at all, where the cut is to be made: then a firm clean cut: that is reverence—if he were dithering with reverence or shuddering or trembling with reverence, he would probably kill the patient.

Note that part of reverence is careful questioning whether one should operate at all: one does not lightly plunge in to remake others. When the decision is for action, then reverence for the essence of man intervenes again. Man's essence is decisive as to the object of our reforming action. It must also guide us as to the process. We must try to restore man to the kind of being he essentially is; and we must try to restore him by means that take account of his nature. If the defect is in the seeing, so that he does not see reality aright, we must try to show him, to help his seeing, not compel him to say that he sees what he doesn't, or psychologically condition him so that he sees whatever we want him to see. If the defect is in the will, we must try to persuade, not brutalize or terrorize or psychologically mutilate him so that we have imposed our will upon his—a wicked thing, no less wicked if we use the most advanced psychological methods to do it kindly. Reverence requires that healing, that is restoring, be the major consideration. There may be occasions when a man so threatens others by the evil in him, that their protection must take precedence of his healing—he may have to be prevented by force from harming them. But here again reverence is the guide: reverence for those to whom he is a threat: reverence for him, once his threat to others is nullified.

So far I have been talking of respect for man because of the essential things in him—the likeness to God, the immortality, the redemption by Christ—which persist no matter how defective each one of us is. But there is a sense in which we must respect men's defects—not as defects, of course, but as facts. We must not act as if they were not there—which is the common fault of the designers of

Utopias. By all means work for the improvement of men, but do not proceed to build your social order as though you had improved them, till you have. A doctor will try to heal a paralyzed leg, but meanwhile he expects the cripple to limp and does not prescribe a set of exercises which includes running. Our Utopia-makers do things as foolish as that. They gaze upon men, one presumes, and see men's defects. Then they construct their systems as though the defects did not exist.

The truth is that all social orders have to be built with defective material. If engineers had only damaged steel to build their bridges with, there would have to be a science of damaged steel. There must be a science of damaged men. Making social orders is like building bridges with defective steel: worse, it is like the building of bridges by defective engineers. For the defects that mar man as social material are present in the planners. We had better leave a margin for them too.

6

Law

(1)

MAN'S PRIMARY RIGHT is to be treated as what he is. We have been looking at what he is. But we cannot study man in a vacuum. He exists in a universe. The universe, not being a chaos, has laws and man is subject to them.

Exploring the universe man discovers more and more of its laws, and, with each new law discovered, his freedom increases. If, at first hearing, this sounds paradoxical, that is only because we are thinking of the laws of the universe, God's laws, as though they were like the laws that man makes. Man's laws constrain us only when they are enacted, so that we may feel each new law as a new interference. But when a scientist, say, announces a law of nature he has not enacted it, but only discovered it. For the laws of the universe are there all the time, and we are affected by them whether we know them or not. We do not need to know about Vitamin B to die of malnutrition for want of it; the new-born baby can be destroyed by the law of gravity as easily as Sir Isaac Newton. So that man's discovery of these laws is not the beginning of his subjection to them; on the contrary, once he knows what they are, he can learn how to co-operate with them, and by so co-operating increase his own freedom within them. His freedom can be only within them, never from them. By discovering the laws of flight, man was able to harmonize himself with them more perfectly, and so gained the freedom of the upper air. The utmost freedom for man lies in co-operation, obedience, harmony with the universe and its laws.

But is the freedom thus gained real freedom or illusory? The answer depends on what we are thus submitting ourselves to, harmonizing ourselves with. If there is a divine Person behind the universe and responsible for its laws, then submission to it is simply submission to Him, and so true freedom and not servitude; for there is no servitude in harmonizing one's mind with a mind of infinite knowledge, one's will with a will of infinite love. But if there is no Person, only the universe and nothing more, then subjection to it is subjection to the mindless and can only be enslavement: we are simply moving about more largely and more comfortably on a longer chain. For a being with a mind there is no freedom, there is only degradation, in harmonizing himself with a mere mechanism, taking his orders from hydrogen and oxygen and such. There is only grotesqueness and indignity in being forced into harmony with things less than ourselves. One way or another all thinkers have told us that we must be in tune with the universe. But why shouldn't the universe be in tune with us? After all, we know what a tune is, and it does not. If we do not believe in God, we must see ourselves performing in an orchestra under a conductor who does not even know that he is conducting, does not even know that he is. There can be no enslavement so total as that of minds to the mindless. And if there be no

Mind behind the universe, then mindlessness says the last word as it said the first. But the mind of God *is* there, and it is with Him that we are to be in tune, in obedience to His laws that we are to find freedom.

(2)

The absolute dependence of freedom upon law known and obeyed applies not only to our relations with the universe, but to the conduct of our own selves in their inmost reality. Man is not the one lawless object in the universe. Man is not a being so universally adaptable that it does not matter what he does or what is done to him, does not matter in what ways he treats himself or others treat him, because he thrives equally well under all possible treatments. Such a being, indeed, is inconceivable. Of any being at all it must be true that some sorts of treatment are good for it and others bad for it, some help it to be more fully itself, some hinder and cripple it. Man is not a chaos any more than the universe is; and as he learns the laws that govern himself, he is freer. The dependence of freedom upon law is invariable.

Looking at man, with no views already formed as to the nature of law, an observer would say that he *is subject* to bodily and mental laws, and that he *subjects himself* to moral laws. The first two, which may roughly be lumped together as physical laws, the observer might see as the statement of how bodies and minds work, so that men would be *wise* to act accordingly. The moral laws he might feel as being in a different category—men thinking that this is what God wants and that it would be *virtuous* to act accordingly. So feeling, the observer would be only partly right. That God's command gives the moral law a new quality that the physical laws have not got is true. But the moral laws are, just as much as the physical laws, statements of how things work.

If you contravene the bodily laws, you will have disease, deformity and death. If you contravene the laws by which the mind works you will be kept from discovering the truth, so that there will be a veil between you and reality; if you collide too hard with them, the result might be insanity. *The moral laws are just as objective.* They are for the handling of the whole man, and for the direction of the whole life, but they are laws all the same—statements that reality is like that, therefore we must act like that or take the consequences. The moral laws, like the physical laws, tell us how to handle ourselves harmoniously with reality. We must not think that whereas physical laws operate with or without our consent, we have a choice about the moral laws: for they are not simply rules that it is virtuous to observe: they too operate. In this matter the position is exactly the same for both. We can treat either set of laws as though it does not exist. But that is the limit of our choice: we have no choice about the consequences in the one or in the other. The law of justice is as much a law as the law of gravity (the latter is more easily discoverable, but not therefore more important—more beneficial in its observance, more catastrophic in its ignoring). Every sort of consequence flows from this. Because each is a law, we cannot *break* either. We can ignore them or flout them, by walking over a cliff, for instance, or stealing: but the law of gravity is not broken in the one case or the law of justice in the other. Both laws continue to operate and it is we who are broken.

Material law or moral law, either way you are living under God's law: and that applies to every creature of God, from the ruler downwards.

From the ruler downwards I say. Moral law is not only moral, it is law. The run of rulers do not realize this, at any rate not all the time. They know that physical laws are what they are and cannot be changed by them, no matter what the emergency. Food nourishes and lack of it starves, night follows day, microbes kill, muscles and minds, unexercised, atrophy. It is exactly the same with the moral law. The mightiest despot cannot drive a Ford car save as Ford made it to be driven. If he wants to drive a Ford car, then like the humblest of his subjects he must study the maker's instructions. God is man's maker and the laws of morality are his instructions for the running of man. They cannot be broken, but they can be ignored, and, with the man as with the car, the ignoring is destructive: this may not immediately appear —there may even be temporary gain—but the result is always loss.

As I have said, it is hard for the ruler to realize that the moral law is law in this sense. It is hard for everybody, because we have so free a choice whether we shall act morally or immorally. All health for men and communities lies in realizing two truths about the moral laws. The first is that they are laws of reality: to say for example that economics has nothing to do with morals is like saying it has nothing to do with physics: it is not simply morally wrong to go against God's laws to gain something for ourselves, it is plain foolishness: we cannot gain by going against them because they are a statement of the way things really are, observing them goes with sanity. The second is that this is not servitude but freedom, for in observing them man is more fully man and not a travesty.

(3)

God's laws for the ordering of man's life are given, promulgated so to speak, in two ways—written into our nature, uttered to us by God or by teachers sent by Him. Both ways are worth study.

The laws of morality, like the laws that govern our body and our mind, are written into our nature. That is to say, God made us with certain powers which can only function properly in the line of the moral law, and certain needs which can only be satisfied by action in that line: just as our bodies are made with the power to digest certain foods, and will only function if fed by them: the moral laws are in man's structure very much as the laws of diet are. If we do not observe the bodily laws, we get protest in the body, stomach-ache for example. If we do not observe the moral laws, we get that protest in the mind, a troubled conscience, which is in fact the protest of the spiritual part of man against misuse, that is to say against action contrary to the moral law which is woven into the very making of man.

Unfortunately neither the body's protest nor the mind's gives us infallible guidance. The body can settle into bad habits and cease to protest, at any rate, vigorously enough to catch our attention. We may, for instance, be eating food of such sort that the body is not fully healthy; but we may feel satisfied enough, especially if we have never known what perfect health is. Nor is the conscience an infallible guide either. In itself conscience is the practical moral judgment of the mind, the judgment the mind makes as to the moral rightness or wrongness of our actions—not their wisdom or unwisdom, be it noted, but something more profound which can only be expressed as ought or ought not. In making this judgment of ought or ought not, the mind's standard is the law of God which is, in the sense already set out, in the very structure of man's nature. But a lot has happened to man's nature since it came new-built from the power of God; and too much of what has happened has damaged it and not perfected it. Men have damaged their natures by misuse, in spite of the protests of conscience, and have settled into certain routines of misuse. So that on all sorts of wrong actions there is no audible protest any more. Some indeed of these aberrations have managed to impose themselves as duties, with conscience active on their behalf. Thus, there have been peoples who, when a man died, slew his wives to bury them with him, and would have thought it shocking not to. Even when conscience speaks loud and clear against some particular wrong action, some matter upon which our nature is still as God made it, we can find philosophies to explain away the protest, so that ultimately it too falls silent. And one way or another we grow comfortable in some at least of our sins. But they are, slowly or quickly, imperceptibly or spectacularly, damaging us all the same.

The second way of learning the laws of morality, by hearing what God explicitly teaches, brings us to the real distinction between physical and moral laws. Physical laws God leaves man to discover for himself; moral laws He tells man—not only tells him what they are, but tells him to observe them: so that His moral teaching is at once information and command. One can see a twofold reason why God should tell us the one set of laws and not the other. For in the first place the moral laws are harder to discover, and in the second they are more essential to be known.

They are harder to discover. For the physical laws, the only problem is to discover what actually is, what actually happens, and the evidence is all here under our noses: it concerns the material universe or the operations of our minds, and any errors we may make about either produce their results in this life, so that man can see them and correct them; and in a general way the story of man has shown a continual progress in their discovery. Whereas the moral laws treat not only of what is, but of what we *ought* to do; and the evidence is not all available—what follows on being right or wrong about the moral laws does not always show in this life so unmistakably that only the blind can miss it: much of it only appears in the next life, so that it does not help us to rectify errors here upon earth.

They are more essential to be known. Their precepts concern the whole man and the direction given to the whole of life, and they involve that thrust of the self which is the dynamic element in human life: if it goes wrong, life goes wrong. How well or ill the body works, how well or ill the intellect works—these things are facts and significant, but not of the same order of significance as the direction the will takes. Ignorance or even error about physical laws need not twist the whole self out of the right relation to God and to other men. You have there all the difference between error, which *must* be involuntary, for obviously no intellect would choose to be in error, and sin, which is wrongness embraced. God teaches us the moral laws because He wants men to be what He made them to be and help others to be so, because He wants the order of reality to be observed and not mocked. And He can make the laws of morality into commandments, precisely because the will is free–only that which has a choice can be commanded.

The teaching of the moral law by God to man has been progressive. It would be outside the scale of this book to give more than the main stages in the progress. In the Ten Commandments God gave to His chosen people, through Moses, the essence of the natural moral law, the law as it might have been discovered by the mind of man from the way God had made man—provided, of course, that man's nature had remained as God shaped it and man's mind had interpreted that nature aright. Fifteen hundred years later Christ restated the law given to Moses, perfected it, and uttered its profoundest meaning in the two commands that we love God with all our power and love our neighbour as ourself. These two commands were not meant to supersede either the great mass of detailed commands for the application of the natural law, or the new precepts that Christ gave–as in the matter of Baptism, for instance–in relation to man's supernatural destiny. But they give us the life principle of all laws, that without which all of them would only be sounding brass and tinkling cymbal. In the two thousand years since, Christ's Church has carried on the teaching work, taking the Ten Commandments to the uttermost ends of the earth, and applying the moral teachings of Christ to the new situations that social, political and economic changes have produced.

Let us pause for a moment upon the two commandments of love. The law given by God has a great mass of detail, and none of the detail is pointless: every element in it has health and wholeness in its observance, disease or deformation in its ignoring. But all the details down to the tiniest are expressions, and in the long run valueless save as expressions, of love. God loves man, and His laws utter His love, the provision He has made for man's well-being—that well-being including the ultimate perfection of well-being, total union with Himself. Man's submission to the laws is not simply a commonsense acceptance of the rules given him by an intelligent Maker, or a grateful obedience to the rules laid down for him by a loving Father. It is even more profoundly a co-operation of man's will with God's will. Love is the reason God gave the laws, love is man's best reason for keeping them: "If you love me, keep my commandments," not "Keep my commandments or it will be the worse for you."

It *will* be the worse for us if we do not keep the commandments. Any contravention of the moral laws damages man, because they *are* laws: one does not have to know the laws of morality to be damaged by coming into collision with them. But the damage is not fatal unless we have broken a command of love—that is, unless we have deliberately chosen love of self as against love of God. That, and only that, makes sin mortal, death-bearing.

7
Love

(1)

THE MORAL LAW, the sum of God's commands for human action, is as various as the ways in which the will of man may thrust wrongly. But all the various commands and prohibitions that it contains are reducible to, or modes of application of, one single principle of action, love. Love God is Christ's first commandment; love your neighbour as yourself, His second. In these two are all the Law and the Prophets. Because this book is concerned with human relationships, I shall concentrate on the second commandment, that we love our fellow-men. As we have already seen, the nature of man demands, and examining man we realize, that we must reverence all men. But over and above that the law of God commands, and listening to Christ we learn, that we must love all men—not simply love the lovable, we should hardly need a command for that, but all men whatsoever: we must love our enemies and do good to them that hate us.

The average man's first reaction is that this is totally unrealistic: it is a nice sentiment, charged with idealism, but impossible: that He should have uttered it shows that Christ was indeed the friend of man: if only He had known men better—as well, say, as we do—He would have known that it couldn't be done. But this is folly. As man, Christ experienced all the possibilities of malice that the heart of man can find within itself, indeed human malice seemed as if driven to new ingenuities at new depths for His destruction. He tells us to love our enemies; and who has ever had enemies like His? And if, as man, Christ knew the cruel possibilities of human nature by experiencing their sharpest edge, this was still only the fringe of His knowledge of man: for Christ was God, and as God He knew the being He had created, knew above all the potentialities in man by His gift, and His own power to aid men to realize them. That we love all men is the command of God, who made us. He would not give us an impossible command.

But what does it mean? Clearly it is not an emotional love that is required of us, to *feel* loving. For the emotions cannot be commanded, though they may be slowly brought under some sort of control. Commands can be addressed only to the will, and in the will love belongs. It may express itself in the emotions, more so or less so according to each person's temperament, but in its own self love is an act of the will. And, as Christ makes clear, the most important element in it is willing the good of other men.

We must, then, will the good of all men, not merely wish it, but will it, will it effectively, will to work for it, will it as we will our own. Observe that Our Lord does not say that we must love our neighbour as much as we love ourselves, but only *as* we love ourselves. The degree of intensity will vary, but the love will be of the same sort. We shall not love others as much as we love ourselves—most people we shall love less, a small handful of people we may love more than ourselves. But towards all men it must be real love, a genuine willing good to them, good in the next life, good in this life.

We have seen that the love Christ commands is not an emotional love. But normally there will be some stirring of emotion, some warmth in it. It is true, as we are so often reminded, that Christ commanded us to love everybody, but gave us no command to like everybody. Yet there is danger here. A strong drive in the will which has no warmth in it at all is psychologically something of a monstrosity, and in practice is very difficult to maintain. We should come to *feel* love for men, as men, and not simply hold grimly to the duty of willing and working for their good. Love, thus felt, adds something specific, something for which there is no substitute, something that reverence does not provide, something that pity not only does not provide but may even betray.

Reverence sees the greatness in men, and bows before it. Pity sees the weakness in men and goes to aid it. But pity can easily tend towards magnification of oneself, an enjoyment of one's own freedom from the weakness we are aiding in the other—the tendency to play at God can insinuate itself to the contamination of almost all virtues. It cannot insinuate itself into reverence, which remains the one absolutely indispensable attitude, towards God and towards man. Yet reverence is not necessarily dynamic; it does not of itself demand warmth. It sees the greatness in another, but is not drawn towards that other. Love does all these things. It is dynamic, it has warmth in it, is drawn towards the other, moves towards him, and not simply to aid his weakness as pity does, but to express our fellowship with his whole self. Indeed, in this fellowship lie the special possibilities of human love. Because men are men and I am a man, I know their problems as I know my own, indeed in some sense they are my own. The modalities differ from man to man, but in essence I know every man's struggle, every man's misery, from inside.

But if there should be some warmth of emotion in our love for all men, there should be no sentimentality. Emotion is a legitimate product of love, sentimentality means that the energy has gone out of it to the point where it is denatured and only a parody. The absolute test as between love and sentimentality is whether we can see another's faults, hate them as faults, not minimize or idealize or romanticize their faultiness, and still love him. After all, we see faults in ourselves, and love ourselves still. With the same clear-sighted love, we must love our neighbour. Love is not something soft and mushy that simply asks to be imposed upon. If a man is a liar or a thief or a murderer, I must love him, just as in the same sad circumstances I should love myself. I must face the fact, I must be prepared to act upon it. Love does not mean, for example, smiling foolishly while murderers murder. If a man tries to kill me, I have a right to resist him; if a man tries to kill some other person, I have a *duty* to resist him. Willing good to all men does not mean leaving some men free to do evil to others—as when a criminal attacks a more decent citizen, or when a nation commits brutal aggression upon another.

But here comes the appallingly difficult Christian paradox. The worst of criminals, the most brutal of aggressors, I am bound to love. Christ says so. And He says not only that, but that I must do good to him. We have to stop him if he violates the laws of God to the harm of other people.

We may even have to kill him—on the gallows or in the electric chair if he is a private criminal, in battle if he is in the army of an aggressor. But we must not cease to love him.

Our first instinctive rejection of this as impossible is partly based upon the false idea of love as purely emotional. We must love a man, even if we have to kill him. That does not mean we must be feeling strong affection for him. It does not necessarily mean *feeling* at all (although one who realizes his duty of reverence and love will probably be stirred emotionally to the very depths of his being by the cruel necessity of actions so hard to reconcile with them). I say it does not necessarily involve feeling. It means something far deeper—that we must still, with all the strength of our will, will him good. By his own act he has made it necessary for us to hurt him, to prevent his attaining something he wants but is not entitled to have. Yet we still will him all the good he has left it in our power to will him. And it is no pious platitude, but the plainest reality, that the eternal good we can still will him is more important *to him* than this earthly life that he forces us to cut short.

We cannot call a command to love our neighbour as ourselves impossible, but we must not think it easy either. Of the two errors, that would be the more dangerous, for it would mean that we had not grasped the magnitude of love—an amiable niceness to everybody was not what Christ made into the second greatest commandment. What we should do is soberly examine it, see how far human nature goes out to meet it and at what point the real difficulty in observing it begins. There is an attitude, half cynicism and half indolence, in which we underrate the average virtue of man. There is immeasurably more love in men than in that mood we realize. Christ says that the ultimate test of love is that a man lay down his life for his friend. But that test all sorts of ordinary men are constantly meeting and triumphantly passing. Soldiers are not exceptional men. Every nation has them in vast numbers. The men who man lifeboats are very much like other men, but they risk their lives and often enough sacrifice their lives, not even for friends but for total strangers. It may be too much to say that the ordinary man's instinct is to love his fellow-men, to the point where he will deny himself for them or even risk his life for them, unless some further element enters to prevent that instinct functioning. But it is closer to the reality of human nature than the assertion that men know only self-interest.

The difficulty begins with the elements, whatever they may be, that do in practice prevent the instinct from functioning. Such elements there must be, for love is not the dominant element in human relationships. The plain fact is that love in this sense stops short when the other man arouses our dislike, by his character or his actions or his principles. To love our enemies, to do good to them that hate us—that is the testing point. Only the exceptional person does it. But Christ commands that we all do it. We shall not do it without some more powerful motive than is provided by simply looking at men. The knowledge that God loves them, all of them, provides a reason: yet, as we saw earlier in the matter of reverence, a reason may be clearly seen by the intellect, yet not stimulate men to act. The one thing that can bring love, like reverence, fully alive is the realization that God loved all men enough to become man and die for them on Calvary.

(2)

One might be disposed to feel that, whether or not the command of love is possible, it is not particularly practical. In fact it is of the first practicality.

St. Augustine's definition of human society remains the only one that will work—a group, large or small, of people united by agreement as to the things they love. As one examines the definition, one moves from thinking it intolerably remote from the actual condition of men to seeing that it is all but a truism. For clearly if there is to be a society at all, the members must be united; and what else can possibly unite men save agreement about the things they love? The members of a Shakespeare society are agreed in loving Shakespeare, or they would hardly bother to come together. The members of a trade union are agreed in loving better working conditions and better pay. The point is not worth labouring. But where the society is concerned with a greater complexity of issues—as a nation is, for example—a new element enters. Agreement in loving the same things does not always unite men, it may even divide them. Agreement to love money, for instance, is bound to divide men, since any money that one man gets another wants, because he loves it. Agreement to love food could divide men to the point of riot and rebellion, if there happened to be a shortage of food. Even agreement to love truth might divide men, if they differed as to what was the truth. There is only one love upon earth which cannot divide but can only unite, and that is love of one another. That is why the command to love our neighbour as ourself is not simply a piece of religion, but the first necessity in human society.

St. Thomas comes at the same truth in another way when he says that where every man seeks his rights, there is chaos. In seeking one's own rights, however determined one is to seek no more than the strictest justice shows to be one's own, there is the certainty that the majority of men will take too large a view of what *is* their own. Over and above that, in our imperfect social orders here upon earth, things are seldom so delicately balanced that everyone can have his own without hindering someone else. Dean Swift defined honour as judging one's own cause as though it were another's, and the definition cannot be bettered. Yet love asks something even harder than honour, that we judge another's cause as though it were our own. This follows as a matter of course if we love another as ourself. We shall be concerned not only with our own rights, but other men's as warmly. Unless there is some principle at work in society ensuring that men shall act thus—or at least see that they ought to—the very foundations of society are fatally weakened. For this is the only answer to the undue thrust of self, which is always liable to destroy the individual character and bring chaos into the social order.

Because the thrust of self is the danger, and because loving others as oneself is the only remedy, it is clear that the element of competition should be kept most carefully in check in any social order that would stay healthy. A competitive system stimulates the thrust of self—if two men are fighting for the same market, in each of them self will have a carnival. And for a man who loves his neighbour as himself, the pursuit of one's own interest to another's loss (which is what the competitive system means) must be painful and ultimately impossible. The usual comment upon this is that without the spur of competition men will not give the best that is in them. But it is not true. The really creative men in any social order—the philosophers, the thinkers, the artists, the scientists—drive themselves mercilessly, without being in competition with anyone. Einstein is not trying to drive some other scientist out of business, Fra Angelico is not trying to outpaint Giotto, Aristotle is not *competing* with Plato. All of them are trying to get at reality and express it. That is their life motive. This may involve correcting the errors of their predecessors, and into this too much of self may enter, and there is always the possibility of too much pleasure in the prestige resultant. But these things are only at the periphery, they are not the driving force. Nor is this absence of competition as a prime motive confined only to men of genius. The majority of men do their work without its spur—teachers, for instance, farmers, sailors, policemen, doctors, judges (to take a handful from a vast number) are not living competitively. I do not say that competition can be wholly excluded from life or that there are no fields in which it is beneficial, but only that it has to be watched most carefully. It *can* stimulate, but it stimulates most those who have no belief in the value of the thing they are doing or making: they get a thrill out of the contest, which other men get out of the exercise of their own best powers upon work well done. What competition infallibly does is encourage the most destructive element in man, the undue thrust of the self.

(3)

Closely related to the necessity for love in human relations is the necessity for trust. Social life is damaged at the source by want of love, and in all its functioning by want of trust. Men love one another too little, but they trust one another hardly at all. And indeed a superficial glance over the human scene does not justify much trust. It rather gives one the feeling that self-interest is the first rule of life as it is lived, and that most people will cheat for it—cheat not only enemies or strangers but benefactors just as enthusiastically. For an idealist, the effort to help his fellow-men might well be heartbreaking. I remember reading of a district infested by snakes, where the local authorities offered a sum of money for every snake's head brought in, and all the farmers began breeding snakes. I may have got the details wrong, for I read it long ago, but whether or not that particular thing happened exactly like that, it is an admirable parable. In one form or another, it is happening all the time. So that an enormous amount of energy—in individuals and in Society as a whole—has to be drained off from fruitful activity into setting safeguards against cheating. All civilized societies are forever building these barriers; and as fast as they are built, men find a way over or under or round them. We have arrived at the fantastic situation where any thinker or statesman constructing a social order, whether as an intellectual exercise or to be brought into concrete existence, plans the barriers first.

I have spoken of what a superficial glance shows; and, what with guarding against being cheated and doing a little cheating on our own account, that is the only sort of glance most of us have time for. But reflection, I think, would show that in this matter we have judged the race too summarily and despaired of it too soon. The facts are beyond question, but human nature is too complex for sweeping judgments. The average man will cheat on his income tax, or do a little smuggling as he passes through the Customs. But the average man will die for the country he is cheating. Which action better expresses the depths of his character? Obviously, the dying. There is so much more weight to that. Is he a patriot or a cheat? A patriot obviously. Then why does he cheat?

There will be two elements in the reason. The ordinary man is capable of heroic sacrifice provided he sees the reason clearly enough; to save his country's existence, he will give his life; but to give the Government a few more pounds or dollars to spend is too small a matter to bring his will to sacrifice alive. That is the first element. The second is his conviction that everybody else is cheating and he does not see why he should be the only one to pay up in full. The vast majority of men would act decently if they saw that the multiplication of small cheatings was producing a universal mistrust from which the whole life of their country suffers damage, *and* if they could be sure that others were acting honestly too. One of the great modern diseases is the terror of seeming to be a sucker. That terror drives all sorts of amiable men into a habit of cynicism, which is very bad for their amiability and indeed very bad for their whole personality. Nothing shrinks the personality so much as suspiciousness.* It is far better to be occasionally deceived than permanently suspicious.

The restoration of trust is essential. But how restore it? Obviously not by passing a law that men shall trust one

* A few years ago, it was decided to test the honesty of school-children in a large area. They were given an examination, consisting of a number of questions to which the answers were Yes or No. Their papers were collected and marked, but no marks put on them. They were

another. It can only be done by working at the two reasons which as we have seen make ordinary men untrustworthy. Take the second first—the conviction that other men are cheating, and why shouldn't oneself? Let us look at oneself. It is not as though you and I were wholly virtuous men in a world of criminals, forced to lower our own standards to theirs that we may survive. We are all sinners, and if we except the saints at one end and abnormally evil men at the other, we are all pretty much at the same level. I have my faults, and you have yours, but my faults are not less faulty for being mine, yours are neither any the worse nor any the better for being indulged in by you rather than by me. We all, more or less habitually,

> Compound for sins we are inclined for
> By damning those we have no mind for.

You commit the sins that tempt you, and I the sins that tempt me. And we all feel virtuous for not committing other people's sins, whereas there is no virtue at all in not committing sins for which one lacks either the temptation or the constitution.

All of this may seem obvious and not worth my saying or your reading. But I think it contains the key we are seeking. A dispassionate examination of ourselves shows that we are much like other people. What is true of us is

---

then returned to the children, the correct answers were read aloud to them, and they were instructed to mark their own. The marks they gave themselves were compared with the marks the teachers had given them, and it was discovered that a large proportion—40% or so—of the children had cheated. What no one seems to have remarked was that 100% of the teachers had cheated—by giving the children to understand that the papers had not been marked. If they managed to avoid actually saying it, their behaviour was not more honourable for that. Suspiciousness is *very* bad for integrity.

probably true of them. Now one thing that is true of us is that although we have all sorts of faults, we are more or less average reasonably decent people all the same. We have all sorts of faults, *but we know that there are things we would not do*. Our own personal code puts them totally out of consideration. Upon them we can trust ourselves, can know ourselves trustworthy. Then why can we not similarly trust others? Because we do not know what they would regard as unthinkable. We have no means of knowing their personal code, and in this mid-twentieth century there seems to be hardly any general code which we may assume that all ordinary men would regard as binding. What is there that we can feel absolutely certain that the man next door would not do? The answers do not spring to mind as readily as one might wish. We are certain that he would not practise cannibalism. What else? The chances are a thousand to one that he would not be guilty of treason. But how certain could one be that he would not break his marriage vows, or take a bribe, or lend money usuriously, or wriggle out of a contract? There is no point in dragging out this curious questionnaire. The point is that we cannot profoundly trust any man unless we know what his moral standards are. What Society needs is a moral code, covering the daily life of man, accepted by the vast majority of its members. It must be accepted as binding, because invested with authority. In practice no authority is strong enough save the authority of God. It is hard to think of any other authority that could be a real check upon the questing selfishness of men. But a moral code thus accepted would remove most of that uncertainty as to how others are likely to act which is one obstacle in the way of trust.

As against the other obstacle, men must be brought to see certain virtues not as pleasing ornaments to life in community, but as essential. That men may live together happily and healthily, they need reverence and love and trust. One's first instinctive reaction is to feel that this is asking for the moon, that men will always grab for money or whatever else will serve their own interests. It may be asking for the moon—though there is daily evidence that men *will* make heroic sacrifices for their fellows. What is certain is that to try to get a decent human society on any lesser terms is asking for the moon too, and even more hopelessly. It will hardly be denied that the love-reverence-trust formula would cure most of our social ills at the root, and remove most of the obstacles to the healthy functioning of men's life in community. Nothing else will do either. So that we must choose between trying for this or despairing of human brotherhood altogether. That would be treason. We must work for the one thing which would be effective if men could be persuaded to try it. And the first step is to try to live by it ourselves. Total success could only be for the saint; but even the effort could work a revolution. And we are not entitled to say that men will not make the effort, when we have done nothing to show them that the effort is worth making.

In this First Section our concern has been Man, not the Social Order. His relations with others have continually come in, but only as incidental to our study of Man and for the light they shed upon him. But in themselves they are not incidental. They belong to man's nature. We should not come into existence unless other human beings produced us, or long stay in it unless they cared for us. Nor is this dependence upon others a humiliating necessity at our origin, which we will in due course outgrow. Full-grown, we are still linked close to others; and not only by our needs as the baby is, but by our powers as well. We have needs which we cannot supply for ourselves—bodily needs, as to be fed and clothed and sheltered and healed from sickness and protected against the violence of stronger men; spiritual needs—some of them easy to list like the need to understand life, met by scholars and philosophers and artists and scientists, to say nothing of theologians, all in their own ways; some easier to see than to formulate, like the need to share joy or sorrow, or our natural movement to be with others, so that we are lonely if left too long without them, and solitary confinement is one of the worst of punishments. And we have powers—to love, for example, to teach, to procreate—which, if any one of us tried to be wholly sufficient to himself, must lie dormant. Save in a vital relation with his fellow-men no man could ever reach maturity: so many needs unmet, so many powers unexercised, he would be a rough sketch for a man, no more. The social relations belong to man's nature *as man* just as his soul and his body and his relation to God belong: so that to the rights we have already seen as flowing from that, must be added the right to associate with his fellow-men.

Man's ways of associating with others can be of an amazing diversity, as anyone may see who pauses a moment to think of the number of people he knows and would be the poorer for not knowing, and the number of groups he belongs to. Of these groups two—the Family and Society—are more important than all others in the natural order, and provide a natural framework of life in which other relationships must find their place. For the others are very much at man's taste and choice, so that he can have more or fewer of them; but as we shall see, Family and Society are rooted in his nature. The rest of the book will be about them.

But from a special point of view. I am not aiming at a full-length treatment of either. The psychological and emotional problems that can arise between husbands and wives, or between parents and children, are not my business here: I am not writing an essay on Marriage Guidance. Nor do I try to draw the blue-prints for the Ideal State. That is quite beyond my competence. In neither field am I trying to solve problems, but only to clarify the principles without which they cannot be solved. Men and women who have grasped the principles may be trusted to build their own family life, without advice from me. A citizen body which has come to accept them as living realities will see for itself where social and political life needs to be re-fashioned. The principles are indispensable, and they are my sole concern here—what the nature of man requires in the two institutions, the tests they must meet if men and women are to be able to live humanly in them.

Of the two, the Family is primary. To Society belongs the job of seeing that man's life on earth is organized, to the Family the job of seeing that human life continues. There would be nothing for Society to organize if people did not continue being born: Society does not beget babies or bear them. We shall treat of the Family first.

MARRIAGE AND THE FAMILY

8
The Nature of Sex and Marriage

(1)

THE TYPICAL modern man practically never thinks about sex.

He dreams of it, of course, by day and by night; he craves for it; he pictures it, is stimulated or depressed by it, drools over it. But this frothing, steaming activity is not thinking. Drooling is not thinking, picturing is not thinking, craving is not thinking, dreaming is not thinking. Thinking means bringing the power of the mind to bear: thinking about sex means striving to see sex in its innermost reality and in the function it is meant to serve.

Our typical modern man, when he gives his mind to it at all, thinks of sex as something we are lucky enough to have; and he sees all its problems rolled into the one problem of how to get the most pleasure out of it. To that he gives himself with immoderate enthusiasm and very moderate success. Success, in fact, can never be more than moderate, because his procedure is folly.

Sex is a power of the whole man, one power among many: and man is not an isolated unit, but bound to his fellows in society: and his life on earth is not the whole of life, but only a beginning. To use the power of sex successfully we must use it in balance with the rest of our powers, for the service of the whole personality, within a social order, with eternity to come. And all this is too complex a matter to be left to instinct or chance, to desire or mood or the heat of the blood or the line of least resistance. It calls for hard thinking.

A summons to think about sex will be met with no enthusiasm. Men are not much given to thought about sex; as we have noted, they expect no fun from thought and are not much inclined to it or good at it: whereas they expect a great deal of fun from sex and persist in thinking (in the face of the evidence) that they are good at it. Not only that. They feel that there is something rather repellent, almost improper, in the association of sex and thinking. A man must be cold-blooded, they say, to use his reason on sex. The taunt of cold-bloodedness is one that we can bear with fortitude. To the man with fever, a normal temperature seems cold-blooded—but vitality goes with normal temperature, not with fever. And modern sex life is not, even by its own standards, very vital. Too many men who have reached middle life have to admit that for themselves sex has not lived up to its promise—that on balance their life has been rather more begloomed by sex than delighted by it. They have had plenty of glowing anticipation, a handful of glowing experiences, a mass of half-satisfactions and whole frustrations—with the horizon drawing in, and the worried feeling that the splendour has somehow eluded them. It is not from any brilliantly successful sexual life of his own, that the typical man of today can deride the idea of using the mind on sex.

Upon sex, as indeed upon all our other powers, we *must*

use reason. Instinct is excellent for the lower animals, but we are not lower animals, we are rational; and the price we pay for our rationality is that reason is our only safe guide, to ignore it is always disaster. There is something pathetic about the philosophers who decry reason and raise the standard of instinct, as about little boys who play at being Red Indians. The little boys would not survive ten minutes in a Red Indian world, the philosophers would perish rather more quickly than the rest of us—for this philosophy has a great attraction for pallid men—in a world of instinct. The instincts that guide the non-rational creature to the fulfilment of his life—to choosing the food that will nourish or constructing the habitation that will shelter or providing for the preservation of his own life and the continuance of his species—do not guide man. All of these things we have to learn. What we call our instincts are natural desires strongly felt—like the instinct of hunger to eat, or of cold to be warmed, or of maternal love to protect, or of gluttony to surfeit, or of sloth to idle, or of pride to rule, or of covetousness to snatch, or of envy to vie, or of anger to kill, or of sex to possess. In themselves they are a mixture of necessary and dangerous: reason must sort them out, evaluate and control them—diminish some, strengthen others. The growth of a world in which men can live as men has been the growth of reason's domination over the instincts—all the instincts, even the instinct of sex. There is no special privilege exempting sex alone from the control of reason. That it is more exciting than the others does not make it less in need of control but more. Any one of them, uncontrolled, can make human life unlivable—sex perhaps more so than the others. Over none of them will reason secure perfect control in the majority of us—certainly not over sex. But there is a world of difference between the man who aims at control though he only partially achieves it and the man who does not. Even partial control, which is all that most *will* achieve, is immensely worth striving for.

Thinking about sex will follow the same lines as thinking about any other thing—what does the law of God tell us, what does the nature of the thing itself tell us. Where the law of God is explicit and clearly known, we have enough for right action without further enquiry. But we should study the nature of the thing even then, as a way of understanding God's law better and of entering into the mind of God who gave the law. In this matter of sex, we shall begin with the nature of man and then go on to the law of God.

(2)

If we consider sex in itself and ask what Nature had in mind in giving sex to human beings, there can be only one answer: Sex is meant for the production of children, as lungs for breathing or the digestive organs for nourishment. The physical and psychological mechanism is so complex in the man and in the woman, so delicately ordered for the generating of new life, that it would be monstrous to deny (nor, one imagines, has anyone ever denied) that that is what sex is meant for, that is why we have sexual powers. The fact that man can use sex for other, sterile purposes of his own choosing does not alter the certainty that child-bearing is sex's own purpose. I know that to the modern reader there seems something quaint and old-world in asking what a thing is for; the modern question is always, What can I do with it? Yet it remains a first principle of the intelligent use of anything to ask what the thing is for—indeed that is almost a first principle of the intelligent misuse of anything. If you are going to pervert a thing, it is wise to know what you are perverting. And to ask what Nature has in mind can hardly be an unnatural opening for any discussion.

But to say that Nature had children in mind when she gave human beings sex does not mean that when two people decide to marry their motive is to have children. If a man draws a girl's attention to the falling birthrate and asks her to marry him in order to improve it, she would be well advised to refuse him: his wooing is a good deal too sociological. People marry, usually anyhow, because they want each other: they may want children too, or they may merely see their advent as probable but regrettable: either way, their purpose in marrying is not to have children but to have each other: and Nature does not mind a bit. She is all for people having their own purposes, provided they do not frustrate hers.

Because custom dulls wonder, dulls advertence even, we hardly realize how extraordinary it is that sex should be for child-bearing. It is extraordinary in two ways. For in the first place it gives a grandeur to sex—a remote and even unwanted grandeur you may feel it, but a grandeur that is incomparable. Against this view of sex stand two very different types. There is the Puritan with his conviction that any activity with such intense pleasure in it must be sinful; and there is the hedonist gathering rosebuds while he may, very fond of rosebuds, indeed, but unable to take them too seriously—there are so many of them and so gatherable: sexual experiences, he will say, are merely thrills in the body, therefore of small consequence. For all their perversions, the paganisms which have centred their rituals upon sex's mystery are nobler than either. The hedonist is denying the plain fact that, even as a bodily experience, the sexual act is like no other, it engages the body more profoundly, at once troubles and concentrates the whole personality in its depth: the excitement of rosebuds is paler. Hedonist and Puritan alike ignore the fundamental relation of sex to the generation of new life, the first fact about sex—that by it man cooperates with God in the production of other men, living beings, immortal beings. Creation is the work of omnipotence. But procreation is pro-creation, a kind of deputy creation. So that sex in its essential nature is man's greatest glory in the physical order.

Sex as men have it, of course, sex existential as we may call it, is not always, or perhaps even commonly, glorious. Which brings us to the second way in which it is extraordinary that sex should be for child-bearing. It is extraordinary because the bearing and rearing of children requires a maximum of order, stability, tranquillity: and sex is the most turbulent of man's powers.

What clouds almost all present discussion of sex is that its demonic energy is not adverted to: the sex reformers write of it as though it were a sort of amiable pet, to be played with and put back in its little basket.

But sex is not like that: in its beauty and ferocity it can be more like a tiger, and even in the mildest it is no domestic pet. Man does not play with sex: it is nearer the truth to say that sex plays with him, and it can be a destructive game. For sex begins powerful and can become uncontrollable. Short of that extreme, it can become a vast tyranny, harrying the individual man, poisoning every sort of human relationship. As I say, the sex reformers seem unaware of this, and probably many of them are so. William Morris is an example. In *News from Nowhere* he chisels this little gem of understatement for us: "For, you know, love is not a very reasonable thing, and perversity and self-will are commoner than some of our moralists think." They are indeed. One gets the feeling that a lot of writing on sex is done by the undersexed—men who honestly cannot imagine what all the fuss is about because in themselves there is no fuss: like the headmaster who wondered why boys could not be taught to discuss their own sexual make-up as calmly as they would discuss the machinery of a motor-car. The early Christian writers—St. Jerome, for instance—repel us by the frenzy of their tirades against women, but at least they knew that there was a frenzy in sex. The frenzy is still there, and anyone who is not aware of it should not write about sex at all.

So we return to our anomaly: the continuation of the race, which requires above all things an ordered framework of life, is entrusted to sex, which of itself makes for chaos. It is in marriage that these two irreconcilables are reconciled. The critics of marriage have simply not realized how incredibly difficult, and how totally necessary, is the reconciliation it effects. In marriage sex loses none of its strength, but it serves life.

But if marriage is to serve life fully—bring the child not only to birth but to maturity—it must be permanent. The new-born child has to be shaped into a fully developed member of the human race; and for this he needs both parents. Humanity is not man or woman, but both in union. A child brought up by a father only or a mother only is only half-educated. He needs what the male can give him and what the female can give him. And he needs these not as two separate influences, each pushing him its own way, so that he moves on some compromise line that is neither, but as one fused influence, wholly human, male and female affecting him as conjoined not as competing influences. For that the parents must be united—and indissolubly united. It is not enough that they should agree to live together only while the children need them—because then they would already be separated in spirit, and their two influences would bear upon the child as two not as one. So that if nature is to solve its problem and reconcile its irreconcilables, to make sex serve life, it needs unbreakable marriage.

Are we, then, to see the love of the man and woman for each other as a trap set by nature to lure them into prison, with every sentence a life-sentence? Are human beings no more than pawns in nature's game of preserving the race?

Nothing could be further from the reality. Men, in nature's plan, are never pawns. They cannot serve nature's purpose without serving their own. In marriage the power of sex is not weakened. Marriage provides strong banks within which sex can course at the utmost of its power, but for the service of life and not for destruction.

There is a common error here—that the great lover is the multiple lover, that sex is made perfect in promiscuity. But it is in the love of one for one that men have always seen sex supremely manifested. Not in Henry VIII or Casanova is sex glorified, but comic, clownish.

And it calls for no long reflection to see why. There is no vitality or mastery in barely being able to totter from one woman to the next, any more than in barely being able to last from one cigarette to the next. There is no mastery in being unable to say no. About the sex-ridden there is a prowling restlessness that is a far cry from vitality. Casual promiscuity is evidence not of sexual potency but only of weakness of control. There is no strength where control is not strong. The phrase sexual impotence is always taken to mean impotence for the sexual act; but there is an impotence before the demands of sex which is entitled to the same name.

Marriage, as the union of one man and one woman, gives opportunity for a splendour of sex impossible outside it, and this both at the level of technique, which does not concern us here, and at the deeper level of personality, which does. The sexual act, merely as a union of bodies, can give exquisite physical pleasure (though it is surprising how often it does not). But it has a double defect.

First, it cannot continue to satisfy even at its own unambitious level: it follows the law of diminishing returns that governs the merely physical pleasures—the dose must be increased to give the same effect. The body craves for the sensation, but after a time grows used to it, is unstimulated by it and craves for more intense sensation. But the act in its essence does not allow for much increase of the dose: so that a man either settles down grimly to a craving he must be for ever yielding to with less and less fruit of satisfaction, or else exhausts his inventiveness in perversions that will for a while bring back the first excitements. It is the universal human experience that a point comes when the craving for the act is overmastering and the pleasure from the act all but nil, so that the act can be neither refused nor enjoyed: that being the way of the body's cravings.

Second, a union of bodies is not the fulness of sexual union. It is valid only as an expression of the union of two personalities. Apart from that, it is a meaningless acrobatic. In other words, the sex act is not the marriage union, but is a marvellous way of expressing the marriage union. When, into the union of bodies, all the shared life and shared love of a man and a woman are poured, then you have the sexual union in its fulness. And in this sense it is no paradox to say that the promiscuous, however many experiences they may have had, remain inexperienced. The giving of the bodies at once symbolizes, expresses, and helps to effect, the giving of the selves. The completer the self-giving, the richer the bodily union. The giving of one's self to another is the decisive act, the act that transforms. While the self is un-given, one remains isolated, singular, single. Those who have never made the gift of self retain, through any number of bodily unions, a sort of unclean virginalness.

But the giving of a self and the receiving of a self, the union of personalities—all these can only in their completeness be of one to one—they belong in marriage, and precisely in marriage that is indissoluble. They are not always found in marriage—we shall be looking at this later—but they are not easily to be had outside it. Where they are found, there is sexual union in its perfection; so that, in falling in with the plan nature has for the carrying on of the race, sex is enriched. The bodily union merely as such—and indeed the whole sexual experience of which it is the normal culmination—can bring a new value into ordinary life, a heightened awareness, an intensification of all vital processes. The thing called glamour is real and valuable. But in marriage as nature would have it all this is increased and given a new hope of permanence. The sexual union has more to utter; and there is not the certainty of ultimate boredom which goes with all purely bodily pleasures. For while one soon comes to an end of what the body has to give, there is no end to the exploration of a personality. So that an act which must become stale when repeated for its own sake, need never become stale when it is regarded as the expression of a profounder reality that is always growing.

Falling in with nature's plan is, then, sheer gain for sex. It is sheer gain for the whole personality. A man and a woman represent, each of them, half of human nature: each needs the other for completion. But the completion will not come from mere contact or cohabitation. There is something here faintly like what happens when two parts of hydrogen are brought together with one part of oxygen: you would expect water, since those are water's constituents: but you will not get it until you send an electric spark through. Humanity is composed of man and woman: but putting a man and woman together does not of itself constitute the true human compound: something else must happen, something electric perhaps. There must be that real giving and receiving we have already spoken of, a free-will offering of the self by each to the other. Obviously you can have marriage where this mutual giving is at the barest minimum; but it is not marriage at its best, and it does not bring the enrichment of personality that each needs. In some marriages it comes quickly, in some slowly, in some hardly at all. But the quality of the marriage is measured by it. Especially is the *permanence* of marriage linked to it. There is no such thing as a permanent union of flesh that is only that. One remembers W. S. Gilbert's young man, who defended his infidelity so eloquently:

> You cannot eat breakfast all day
> Nor is it the act of a sinner
> When breakfast is taken away
> To turn your attention to dinner.
> And it's not in the range of belief
> That you should hold him as a glutton
> Who when he is tired of beef
> Determines to tackle the mutton.

It could not be better put. Modern sex life is a series of quick-change acts, hardly more emotionally significant than tiring of beef and tackling mutton. To ask for life-long fidelity where there is no union of personalities really is to ask for the moon.

9

Marriage and the Law of God

(1)

THE BIBLE, which has a marriage in the first chapter, is shot through with intimations of God's will upon sex and marriage. In its main lines His teaching is to be found in the Old Testament; Christ Our Lord developed and clarified this in His time upon earth, and has continued to teach it through His Church in the twenty centuries since.

Broadly it may be summarized in two statements: that the powers of sex must never be used outside marriage; and that marriage is monogamous and unbreakable save by death.

Consider first the restriction of the use of sex to marriage. This involves two consequences: sex must only be used between a man and a woman: and only within the framework of a legal union. Concubinage was tolerated among the chosen people for a long enough time, but it had disappeared before the coming of Christ: and concubinage was, in any event, a state recognized and regulated by law: it was not casual intimacy, still less mere promiscuity: for neither of these has Scripture a moment's tolerance. A man and a woman must not unite their bodies merely at their choice but only within the framework of a legal union: no union of bodies, or any use of the sex organs, was in any circumstances thinkable save between a man and a woman—not by either alone, or in union with another person of the same sex, or with an animal. Christ Our Lord simply took over these laws, adding one profound development—for He taught that sex might be misused even in the mind, apart from any outward act—the man that looks after a woman to lust after her has already committed adultery with her in his heart. The Church has had nothing to clarify here or make in any way plainer. Nor, if what has been said in the last chapter seems to make sense, is it hard to see the reasonableness of this total restriction: it enables the sexual powers to do what they are there for: and to be most fully themselves. Only within marriage do the powers of sex serve the new life by which the race is continued. For only from the sexual union of a man and a woman can children be born, obviously sex's primary purpose; only in their legal union is the ordered framework of life possible in which the children can be reared to maturity. And in marriage, as we have seen, sex can attain its own maturity as an expression of the total union of two personalities.

So we come to the second great law—the law of marriage as the union of one man with one woman till death (as with concubinage, so with polygamy; Christ tells us that Moses allowed it because of the hardness of men's hearts, but He Himself restored the original law). Here the teaching of the Church holds a very delicate but quite essential balance between fixity and freedom. Marriage is an institution whose nature and laws do not depend upon man's choice. Marriage is what it is: God made it what it is because thus it is best for the human race. Man cannot alter it: he can only take it or leave it. And in that precisely lies his freedom. He can take it or leave it. A man or a woman cannot be forced to marry: either is morally free to marry or not to marry (and of course either is physically free to enter into *any* sort of living arrangement with the other). We can choose whether or not to marry: but we cannot choose what marriage is. The Church expresses all this in the statement that marriage is a relationship resulting from a contract: the contract is made by the man and the woman, the relationship that results is made by God. The man and the woman agree to take each other as husband and wife for life: God makes them so, taking them at their word.

Thus the laws relating to marriage fall into two divisions—laws about the contract, laws about the relationship.

Consider the *contract:* a man and a woman agree to marry. There are two key words here—*agree* and *marry*. Their agreement must be unforced, otherwise it is not an agreement at all: prove that either of them was compelled, and the contract vanishes. Similarly it must be an agreement to *marry,* that is to enter into a union for life, to the exclusion of all others, a union that is meant by God to produce, and normally will produce, children. If they enter into an agreement to take each other for a term of years, or till one or other wearies of the arrangement, or to the total exclusion of children—then it is not a contract to marry. Prove any of these things and the contract vanishes. There are other ways in which what looked like a marriage contract turns out not to be one (as, for example, if either is married already, or is impotent, or if the due form is not observed), but the two we have dwelt on illustrate the principle best. Before God brings the relationship called marriage into existence, the man and woman must have made a contract to marry. Where it can be shown that a given couple have not done so, the competent authority will grant a decree of nullity. Where they *have* done so, there is a marriage. God has brought the relationship into being. If marriage were only a contract, it would, like all other contracts, be breakable by the agreement of both parties to it. But it is not. Once they have made their contract, the parties are bound, not by it, but by the relationship that follows. Let us look more closely at this relationship.

God has taken a man and a woman at their word. They are now husband and wife, made so by God. They are not simply a man and a woman who have agreed to live together for certain agreed purposes. If that were all, they would have entered into an arrangement; but marriage is not an arrangement, it is a relationship. It is hard to make this clear, though once one has seen it nothing could be more illuminating. A man adopts a son: that is an arrangement. A man begets a son: that is a relationship. In marriage the man and woman have not simply adopted each other as husband and wife, in the way a man adopts a son. They *have become* husband and wife, God has made them so. They are united, not simply by an agreement to be so, but by some vital reality. The relationship of husband and wife is not brought into being in the same way as the relationship of parent and child, for the latter arises in a union of bodies, the marriage relationship in a union of wills: but it is all the closer and more real for that. A husband and wife are not less vitally and really related to each other than they are to their own children, but more.

Our Lord makes His own the phrase of Genesis which puts this fact with dazzling clearness: "they shall be two in one flesh." In the nineteenth chapter of St. Matthew's Gospel we find him saying to the Pharisees: "A man therefore will leave his father and mother and will cling to his wife and the two will become one flesh. And so they are no longer two they are one flesh: what God, then, has joined, let not man put asunder." In the fifth chapter of his epistle to the Ephesians, St. Paul quotes the same phrase of Genesis, leading up to it by a figure of speech which at once re-asserts the new oneness that marriage has brought into being, and lays its foundation deeper than the natural eye of man can pierce: for he compares the union of a man and his wife with the union of Christ and His Church. "Wives must obey their husbands as they would obey the Lord; the man is the head to which the woman's body is united, just as Christ is the head of the Church, the Saviour on whom the safety of his body depends. Why then, women must owe obedience at all points to their husbands, as the Church does to Christ. You who are husbands must show love to your wives, as Christ showed love to the Church when he gave himself up on its behalf . . . and that is how husband ought to love wife, as if she were his own body; in loving his wife, a man is but loving himself . . . That is why a man will leave his father and mother and will cling to his wife and the two shall become one flesh. Yes, these words are a high mystery and I am applying them to Christ and his church."

There is something in the modern temper, of the Western world at least, which is so jarred by the opening phrase "Wives must obey their husbands"—that we do not read on to the vastly exhilarating truth that follows and, if we do, are not exhilarated by it. The phrase seems to sum up appallingly all that business of masculine domination from which women feel they have fought free. But it certainly does not mean that. The woman's duty of obedience is balanced by the man's duty of love: she is to be obedient, not to a sultan issuing ukases, but to one who loves her as himself. The model is the obedience of the Church to Christ, and Christ is not tyrannical; Christ commands, but gives love, not fear, as the reason for obedience—"If you love me, keep my commandments." Further, the Church has clarified the obedience due. In the encyclical *Casti Connubii,* Pope Pius XI writes: "This subordination, however, does not deny or take away the liberty which fully belongs to the woman, both in view of her dignity as a human person, and in view of her most noble office as wife and mother and companion; nor does it bid her obey her husband's every request if not in harmony with right reason or with the dignity due to a wife. In short, it does not imply that the wife should be put on a level with those who in law are called minors, to whom it is not customary to allow free exercise of their rights on account of their lack of mature judgment or of their ignorance of human affairs. What it does is to forbid the exaggerated liberty which has no care for the good of the family; it forbids that in this body which is the family the heart be separated from the head to the great detriment of the whole body and the proximate danger of ruin. For if the man is the head, the woman is the heart, and as he occupies the chief place in ruling, so she may and ought to make her own the chief place in love."

The family is a society, and someone must have the final word, otherwise nothing is ever decided but all is in permanent debate. An endless tug-of-war is a miserable business. Nor would it be for the good of family life if the question of headship should be settled in each family by a contest of personalities, won in some families by the man, in some by the woman. It is not a question of men being superior to women—the need any society has for an authority to order it aright does not mean that those who wield the authority are in any way at all superior as persons to those who obey it. In secular society Queen Elizabeth, for example, was not greater than her subject, Shakespeare; in the Church, Gregory IX was not a holier man than his subject Francis of Assisi. The wielding of authority is a function, a necessary function, giving no reason to feel proud, any more than obedience to it gives reason to feel humiliated.

That the father is the head of the family does not mean that the mother cannot exercise authority: both must be honoured. And that the mother is the heart of the family does not mean that the father need not love: he, who must love his wife as Christ loves His Church, does not suddenly shut off all love to the children born of his love for her. Both wield authority and both love, but the emphasis is different. And there is a similar unity with difference in the matter of training the child. The father's part is indispensable; but in all the earlier years the mother has the main contact with the child. Its attitude to life it must learn from her. She is the custodian of the standards—standards of manners, standards of morals—

of what is right and wrong, good and evil, permissible and forbidden, tolerable and intolerable. If she does not teach these things, the child will not be taught. In all the Christian centuries, the task has been simple enough. The mother had merely to hand on to her children what had been handed on to her. But in our own century that is changed. The world into which the child is to go from her will deride the moral standards—not merely disobey them as people at all times have, but deny their validity. The mother now who would do her duty as custodian must tell her children not only what the standards are but why they are, must arm them with that understanding of the real universe in which the moral laws will be seen for what they are, and the world's assault upon them for what it is.

(2)

In entering into this union, each has given to the other (and to the other exclusively) the right to sexual union. Notice that sexual union is a thing due, a right: either is entitled to demand it of the other and, unless there is a very serious reason, neither can refuse it to the other. For the man to refuse his wife or the wife her husband without good reason would be a grave sin. But notice that it is a right, not to *any* sexual union but to normal sexual union, the union by which, in the way of nature, children are conceived. Abnormal sexual unions are forbidden to the married as to everyone else; abnormalities in the normal sexual union—all the ingenious trickeries that interfere with it to prevent children being conceived

—are likewise forbidden. The sexual act must be wholly itself.

And the right thus given is no merely legalistic right—a mere right to the use of the other's body for a specified purpose. The will must go with it; as far as possible—it is not always possible, the feelings cannot be commanded—the whole personality must go with it. The marriage act is a duty, certainly, but this is one duty that cannot be done simply as a duty: it must be done generously or it is not being done at all. It can never be repeated too often that the sexual union is not simply a union of bodies; it is a union of personalities, expressing itself in the union of bodies. But precisely because the bodily union has so splendid a function, it should itself be splendidly performed. There is a technical competence to be learned by each, for this is an action not of each individually but of two in unison; each surrendered totally to the rhythm of the other. Where it is rightly done, there is an exquisite physical pleasure for both, for so God has made man and woman. Both are meant to experience this pleasure—each must strive that the other may have it. In its fulness the act not only expresses the union of personalities, the total giving of the body uttering the total giving of the self, but intensifies and enriches it. Where there is any want of generosity in the act by either, the union of personalities is impoverished.

It is interesting to observe how the Church, pictured often enough as the enemy of sex, insists upon all this.

In his widely read book, *Pardon and Peace,* the Passionist Father Alfred Wilson lists some questions that husbands and wives might ask themselves to test how far their sexual life together approaches the ideal: the first two are especially for wives: "Have I habitually failed in my duty, by giving to intercourse only a reluctant and condescending acquiescence, and by my grudging attitude largely destroyed the value of such acquiescence?"

"Have I been selfish in the refusal or performance of intercourse? Consulted only my own mood and never attempted to accommodate myself to my partner's mood or done so only with the pose of a martyr to duty?"

For men: "In the preliminaries of intercourse have I nauseated my wife by my complete failure to show a delicate and sensitive consideration for her feelings and desires?"

"Do I realize that whilst the biological purpose of intercourse is procreation, the psychological purpose is the expression and preserving of a unique love?"

"Have I raised my mind to God during intercourse and humbly thanked Him for this pleasure, this sacramental expression of love . . . or have I instead considered myself 'outside the pale' and mentally skulked away from His presence and His love?"

The Church, then, sees that the health of marriage requires a positive attitude to sex. It must be wholeheartedly accepted as God's plan for the continuance of the race; its pleasure must be accepted simply and frankly and with all gratitude to God, by whose will it is there. Which brings us to the other element in the Church's thought upon marriage. Just as there must be a positive attitude to sex, so there must be a positive attitude to God. A negative attitude to either is corrosive. God must not be seen primarily as someone we can offend, or sex primarily as something we may misuse. But God must be seen as the fount of life and of love, sex as a channel of life and of love.

Why single out God and sex in this way? Because it is precisely by the lack of a full and positive acceptance of one or other that marriages otherwise healthy most often fail. Marriage itself is the union of two lives, a man's life and a woman's life. Now most people conceive this relation of a man to a woman positively enough—not as a set of prohibitions to be obeyed or pitfalls to be avoided but as love, joy in each other, a mutual self-giving, a certain completion of each by the other, willingness for sacrifice. All this is right and human, essentially healthy and vitalizing. It needs no particular discussion because, as I have said, most people see marriage like that. But what most people do not see is that it can stay like that only if both God and sex are rightly understood and wholeheartedly accepted.

The trouble is that people feel instinctively that there is some sort of incompatibility between God and sex, so that to the believer it seems irreverent, and to the unbeliever at least incongruous, to mention them together. Thinking that they cannot well choose both, people tend to opt for one or the other. Those who opt for sex, leave God wholly out of their picture of marriage; those who choose God, while they cannot leave sex out, admit it in a shuffling shamefaced way, as though wondering what God can possibly think of them!

Thus one may ignore God for the sake of sex or belittle sex for the sake of God. Either way marriage is less vital than it should be. Consider the greater error first—the concentration upon sex to the ignoring of God. To ignore God means quite simply that no part of life is seen rightly or can be lived rightly. God made all things, His will is the only reason why they exist, what He made them for is their only purpose. Leave God out and you leave out the reason for everything and the purpose of everything. We cannot be right about life if we are wrong about God; but we cannot be right about marriage if we are wrong about life. Marriage is seen out of its context if life is seen wrong; sex is seen out of its context if marriage is seen wrong. Out of its context sex, as a union of bodies, or even as a union of persons, looms larger than it should; and is expected to yield a fruit of happiness and human satisfaction which by itself it was never meant to yield, which it is simply not big enough to yield.

Consider now the lesser error—the belittling of sex for the sake of God. This error is more likely to affect Catholics, if and in so far as they lack a positive attitude to God and to sex. It is the feeling that there is something shady about the sex appetite and its satisfaction—that God allows it but looks the other way. But this is to fail to see the glory of the power in itself. By the use of it man co-operates with the creative power of God. The sexual act is not something invented by man's lust and tolerated by God: it is ordained by God Himself as the means for the continuance of man's race. Nor did God plan it as a strictly mechanical means for the production of new life, to be performed dutifully and without elation, for it was God who attached the physical ecstasy to it, so that it is not only a channel of life but a channel of love too.

But their sexual life will only be all that it should be in the life of husband and wife if each grasps fully the meaning both of the act and of its pleasure, and strives wholeheartedly for that competence in it and joy in it which each is entitled to expect from the other. There is of course danger here as there is in all life. The physical pleasure can become overmastering: there can be excess within marriage as well as outside it. The remedy for this excess—as indeed also for that distrust of the physical side of marriage which is the opposite error—is to relate sexual life to God, to thank Him for so good a gift (as Chesterton says we should thank Him for wine) by moderation in the use of it, and to offer it to Him for sanctification as naturally as the rest of life is offered. There is, as Wingfield Hope says in *Life Together,* "an irrational instinct to keep our sex life segregated from God—if sex life side-tracks from God, it may ruin the happiness of any marriage. We must not leave God out of any part of our married life, or of any of our thought on marriage."

That sex is not outside the pale of spirituality God has shown, as we have already seen, in making the marriage union a symbol of the union of Christ with His Church; He has shown it even more startlingly in making marriage a sacrament. For a sacrament is a means of grace, and grace means an energizing of God's life in the soul of man, in its first initiation establishing, and in its increase intensifying, the union of the soul with the Blessed Trinity. Every marriage is a relationship whereby God makes the man and woman one flesh; but to the marriage of the baptized, a greater glory is added. When a baptized man and a baptized woman marry, they receive the sacrament, whether they know it or not; the union with each other, which reaches down to the deepest and most radical urgency of their body, enriches their union with God Himself in the spiritual depths of the soul. Grace is the highest effect of Matrimony, as of any sacrament. But in

Matrimony the sacrament works outward as well, to vitalize the whole relationship. To quote *Casti Connubii:* "The sacrament perfects natural love . . .", again, "the husband and wife are assisted not only in understanding, but in knowing intimately, in adhering firmly to, in willing effectively and in successfully putting into practice, those things which pertain to the married state, its aims and duties."

From all this it should be clear that it is from no undervaluing of sex and marriage that the Church teaches that Virginity is higher and holier still—not any virginity, be it noted, not the virginity of the impotent or the timorous or the reluctant or the uninterested or the otherwise occupied, but the virginity which is a dedication to God of vast energies of love, which but for this higher dedication would have found their issue in marriage. Indeed it would seem that the primacy of such dedicated virginity is one great bulwark of marriage. Marriage is most honoured where virginity is honoured still more. For both are expressions—at two levels, one high, the other higher—of the same truth that sex is a gift of God: men can profane it, but there is no profanation in it save such as men import into it.

(3)

In truth the Church is a puzzle to anyone who does not grasp the principles on which she is thinking in this matter. On the one hand she seems so niggardly about sex—no intercourse outside marriage, no contraception, no divorce—and on the other hand she sees so much splendour in it. But there is no contradiction. Alike in her glorification of sex and in her prohibitions there is one guiding principle. Sex must be itself. It is sex being wholly itself and fulfilling its own function that she glorifies. All the things she prohibits are ways of denaturing the sexual act or cutting it off from its evident purpose.

The act is itself when the bodily organs of husband and wife are properly in contact throughout, and the seed is allowed to take its natural course. It is denatured when and if these conditions are lacking. In solitary vice, for instance, there is no contact because the act is of one person alone. In homosexuality, there is no union of a man with a woman. Even when there is a man and a woman and an approximation to the sexual act, the contact may be broken before the act is complete, or artificial barriers may be introduced so that the organs are not properly in contact at all—the result being that the seed is prevented from going its natural way, the object being to have the pleasure of sex without the risk of generation. Upon all this the Church is adamant. She insists upon the integrity of the sexual act: the act must be wholly itself, it must be allowed to have its natural consequences. To deform or denature it is to degrade it; and to degrade an act of that vital significance is to damage man far beyond the measure of any suffering it is intended to alleviate.

The Church, then, insists that the sex act be not performed, save in its integrity. Equally she insists that it be not performed outside marriage. By the one insistence she safeguards the act itself, by the other she safeguards its function. Her teaching here is wholly in accord with the line of reasoning sketched in the previous chapter. The power of sex is aimed, obviously, at the generating of children. It can serve other purposes, too—at the lowest level it can give pleasure, at the highest it can at once express and intensify the union of personalities—but these other purposes must not be sought in a total divorce from its direct function, the continuation of the race. The institution in which sex best serves this aim is, we have seen, marriage—and indissoluble marriage, the permanent union of the father and mother. Where there is no union at all between the parents, the child is in a desperate insecurity; where there is a union, but not permanent, a union with divorce and remarriage seen as an ever-present possibility, the child's training towards maturity and full membership of the human race will be profoundly damaged. Marriage is the one condition in which the main purpose of sex is secured. The sexual union belongs in marriage and only there.

This is not to say that husband and wife must intend every act of sexual union to be procreative, but only that when they do have sexual union they shall have it in its integrity. They may know that procreation is impossible—for instance, because there is a child already in the womb, or because the wife has passed the age of childbearing. They may feel that procreation is undesirable—because of great danger to the wife's health or a desperate economic situation—and therefore restrict the act to times when conception is improbable. Provided they have the union in its integrity, not deforming or distorting or mutilating it, doing nothing to interfere with the course of nature, then they are within their rights. Such uses of sex still serve sex's primary purpose: they serve the children already born, by making the marriage a firmer, warmer, lovinger thing; if no children are, or can be, born, they still serve sex's primary purpose, for they help to add one more strong and happy marriage to the whole institution of marriage, and it is upon the institution of marriage that the new-born generations depend.

Thus it will be seen that the Church's object is not, as sometimes supposed, that families should have as many children as possible; her concern is that a power so supremely valuable as sex should not be played with. Children, if one may say a thing so obvious once more, have to be not only brought into the world, but brought up in the world; and upon this, as upon all else, men must use their reason. To bring into the world twice as many children as father and mother are financially competent to support, and physically or psychologically competent to handle, is not necessarily to make the right use of the power of sex. A given couple may feel the certainty that it is God's will that they take no thought of such factors and rely upon Him to help them no matter how many children may come. But short of such a special vocation, husband and wife may, as we have seen, decide that there is deeply serious reason for not having another child— for the moment, perhaps, or even in any foreseeable future.

The reason must be serious. Trifles are not enough. That the birth of other children might mean riding in a less expensive car or sending the children to a less fashionable school would not justify the decision to have no more: for that would be making the ornaments of life more valuable than life itself, and not only could no Christian see things so, but only the devitalized could. Indeed for one who has grasped what a human being is— made in God's image, immortal, redeemed by Christ—

only the most serious reason would be strong enough to support such a decision. But where such serious reason exists husband and wife may agree to abstain from sexual intercourse, for a time, or permanently. Or they may agree to have it only at times when conception is most unlikely. In all this there is no want of trust in God, but simply an awareness that in the procreation of children human beings have a necessary part to play, and that they must use their judgment prayerfully as to how they shall play it.

The denaturing of the marriage act is one of the two modern assaults upon the integrity of marriage; divorce is the other. The arguments for divorce are all too obvious. A marriage is a failure, humanly speaking irredeemable. It is causing great mental suffering, perhaps bodily suffering too, to husband and wife. The Church teaches that in such circumstances the suffering party may withdraw and live apart: but may not remarry while the other party lives, for the marriage itself cannot be broken. It is a hard teaching, and to the generality of men seems even repulsive. For two people in the prime of life thus to be condemned to celibacy, especially after marriage has fully aroused them sexually, can mean sheer anguish. Anyone with much experience of life has met case after case where his whole soul longed that the law might be different. The suffering caused is so great a thing, the way of relief seems so small a thing.

But the way of relief is not so small a thing. For it is impossible. It was not through any defect of love that Christ said "What God has joined together let not man put asunder"—Christ, who was so totally love that men who know nothing else about Him know at least that He loved all of our race as it has never been loved.

God makes the man and woman to be husband and wife: no one but God. Neither the State, nor the man and woman themselves with all their striving, can unmake the relationship God has made.* If there is cruelty in the refusal to permit divorce and remarriage, it is not the Church's cruelty, but God's. And God is love.

Somehow, this law, like every law of God, must serve love. The suffering which the law may cause must be outweighed by a greater good for man and a greater suffering avoided. And, in this matter, however much our hearts may be wrung by the sight of individual anguish, the greater good, the balance of advantage, is not hard to see.

The happiness of society as a whole, of the generality of men and women—and still more of children—is bound up with the health of marriage: it provides the one stable framework, the underlying security, without which men and women, and children still more, feel the wretchedness of their insufficiency. Where a given marriage is unhappy, this wretchedness falls upon the individuals concerned: and there are marriages where one feels that everyone concerned, even the children, might be the gainers for ending them and letting the parents start afresh with new partners. One need not stay here to observe that the second marriage is not necessarily much happier than the first—the innocent party may have contributed to the first failure, and in the same innocence will bring the same defects of character and personality to make their modest contri-

* God teaches, through His Church, that there are two instances in which marriage, solidly contracted, may be broken. The first is when the marriage has not been consummated: for good reason, the Church can terminate it. And there is the situation envisaged by St. Paul (I Cor. vii. 15): two unbaptized people marry and later one of them is baptized: if the unbaptized one refuses to live with the baptized (or makes life together impossible), the baptized one may marry again.

bution to the failure of the second. But this is beside the point. The suffering caused to individuals by a marriage that fails is a trifle compared to the suffering caused throughout society by the breakdown of marriage itself.

And unhappily there is no way of breaking individual marriages without damaging the institution of marriage. For any human power to break a marriage because it is unhappy means that marriage as such is breakable; and if marriage as such is breakable, then anybody's is, everybody's is. No two people are any longer united in a relation permanent in itself, but only in an arrangement dependent upon whim or mood or feeling or the thousand chances of life. The institution of marriage no longer exists and society has taken a first step on the road to chaos.

This is not a rhetorical exaggeration. The Church knows, and seems to be alone in knowing, that wedges have thin ends. The world always points to the thinness of the wedge's point of entry, and accuses the Church of making a fuss about a trifle: what harm, says the world, can possibly come from admitting an exception and granting relief in a case so poignant, and happily so rare? The Church sees the thickness of the wedge that lies behind that thin edge, awaiting entry. "To do a great right, do a little wrong" is a plea that the modern man finds irresistible. But there is no such thing as doing a little wrong: the smallest yielding of principle, for however good a cause, is a hole in the dyke and you will not keep out the sea. There is a principle, for instance, that innocent life may never be taken. Of course, says the world: but to save the life of a mother, one may surely destroy the infant within her. The Church is seen to be unyielding and is thought to be heartless—even her own members might wish her to yield a little to common humanity. The Church does not yield. She has her own principle, that God does not allow it. But she knows also about the end and the wedge. Once conceded that innocent life may be taken for so very good a cause, there is no limit to the causes which will seem good enough to justify taking it. Millions of Jews exterminated in lethal chambers are a reminder that she is not being fanciful.

So in our present enquiry on marriage and divorce: the thin end of the wedge was adultery. It was argued, from a text in St. Matthew's Gospel, that Christ allowed divorce and remarriage on that one single ground: I do not thus interpret the text, but I can see how one might. So divorce came in, for adultery. A great deal of wedge has entered since that thin breach was made, and we have not seen the whole of it yet. Roughly speaking, anyone who wants a divorce can have it. He still has to ask for it, and may have to do a little legal manoeuvring for it. But he can get it. There is something else. The mere possibility of divorce helps marriage to fail. The average modern couple enter upon marriage, assuming it terminable, though they have no intention that theirs shall terminate. But successful marriage is not automatic. It has to be worked for, and there are trying moments, as we shall see in the next chapter, as indeed you can see in the life around you. There are difficulties from within—two imperfect personalities to be somehow adjusted; difficulties from outside—economic circumstance, the superior seductiveness of strangers. Marriage, like all other valuable human things, calls for strong efforts and strong resistances: and people who know that marriage is unbreakable, will make them: people who regard it as breakable, won't.

The principle of the end and the wedge has had a spectacular illustration in the matter of birth control. The thin end of the wedge was the wife who would certainly die if she had another baby: to oppose contraception for *her* made one feel like a brute. The wedge made its entry: and the widening was dazzling: till now a high school girl might feel socially inadequate without her contraceptive package. For everybody, married and unmarried, contraceptives seem to have taken the danger out of sex! One can indulge sexual desires irresponsibly, for "nothing can happen." With contraceptives, one feels, sex can be played with. But sex is never to be played with, it is too strong: and something is always happening in the depths of the psyche. The truth is that a healthy use of sex cannot co-exist with *any* deformation of the sexual act, there is too much possibility of frenzy in it; the institution of marriage cannot co-exist with divorce, for human indolence and waywardness will always take the line of least resistance. Any exception upon either abandons the principle, and nothing is left but the wreckage.

All this may seem fanciful to those who regard sex as a life all its own, not related to the rest of life, or as a private hobby with no effects upon the other elements of the individual's life or the life of society—a hobby like stamp-collecting, only more exciting. Such people tend, too, to the romantic notion that you only have to leave sex uncontrolled to get happiness. One wonders how either notion could survive adolescence. Maturity sees sex yielding less happiness today than it ever did, the framework of married life everywhere corroded, the children of broken homes growing into a national problem.

Health for the individual and for society is not simply

a question of the best distribution of material goods—pleasant work, pleasant home, economic sufficiency, sexual desire hollowing its own happy channels. All that is three-dimensional, and man has a strange fourth dimension—the sacred. Life must be sacred, sex must be sacred, marriage must be sacred. For all three there is no sure middle ground between sacredness and profanation. All three run too deep into the heart of reality for a decent respectability to be sufficient or even possible. We have already noted that what man does not reverence he will profane. He must re-learn reverence for life and for sex and for marriage. They can flourish only as sacrosanct.

(4)

In the last section I have talked exclusively of divorce and birth control; and indeed our presentation of marriage to the world concentrates so much on these that an outsider might be pardoned for thinking Christian marriage no more than an heroic refusal to get divorced, accompanied by a tight-lipped renunciation of contraceptives. But these two are diseases of marriage, comparable in the moral order to cancer and consumption in the material. Freedom from cancer and consumption does not mean that a body is healthy; freedom from divorce and birth control does not mean that a marriage is healthy. A body may be free from major diseases, yet unhealthy and devitalized: so may a marriage. To understand health, we must study health—the conditions in which a thing is most fully itself and most abounding in vitality. This study must always be primarily positive. The study of disease—even the recognition that it is disease—comes after.

To summarize all this, the love of husband and wife can be the magnificent thing it is meant to be only if both are living mentally in the real universe, a universe which exists solely because God wills it and in which each thing is healthily itself only by being as God wills it. Men must see what they are and where they are before they can see with real understanding, and not simply by blind obedience, how they should act. And save in relation to God they cannot see what they are and where they are, for save in relation to God they would not be at all. Once a man has this view of reality as a whole, he will scarcely need arguments against divorce and contraception; until he has it, he will not be convinced by them. This bringing in of God is not mere religiosity: it is the plain fact of things. It may seem vastly troublesome to teach men about God before dealing with their concrete problems, but the sooner we realize that the concrete problems cannot be solved without God, the better for everybody.

10

Marriage Existential

MARRIAGE as the nature of man needs it, marriage as God ordains it, harmonize admirably with each other, as we have seen, but a deal less admirably with marriage as men and women actually live it. Reading the last two chapters, the average married couple might smile cynically or even savagely: one can hear them in derisive recitation of the Christian statement of what marriage is—a man and woman made one by God, a sexual life meant both to express the oneness and to bring children into being, he the head, she the heart. Derisively recited, even soberly studied, it sounds unrealistic, hothouse stuff, not for our weatherbeaten world. Not many marriages look much like that; many look like a parody of it. But every marriage, whatever it may look like, is in fact that, just as man, whatever he may look like, is God's image. Husband and wife *are* one, though they may no longer will oneness but turn their every energy to rending, not union; sexual life has those purposes, though the two may pervert it; the husband is the head and the wife the heart, though neither functions. We are about to look at Marriage Existential, as we have already looked at Man Existential. In neither instance are we turning from ideal to real: man and marriage remain, in their essential reality, what we have shown them to be; whatever misuses there may be are misuses of that reality; the misuses are real, certainly, but so is the nature of the thing misused.

There are marriages that start well enough and are wrecked by circumstance, and marriages that seem doomed from the start. The father may be out of work, there may be no houses to be had, so that overcrowding and underfeeding make mock of God's design; husband or wife may die while the marriage is still young. Or the husband may totally lack will-power, the wife totally lack feeling, one or the other may be an alcoholic, or unnaturally cruel or sexually perverted. These are tragic possibilities, but they are not in the nature of the case—they arise, when they do arise, from exceptional circumstances or abnormal characters. They are to be laid more to the count of circumstances and characters than of marriage. When they do occur, it will be cruelly difficult for one or both to rescue what can be rescued. Even then, a grasp of the nature of God and man and marriage and a living, tenacious trust in all three—or even a plain human clinging to the preservation of the family—can bring success where every sign said ruin; and this is not simply optimistic assertion, but a truth verified over and over again in human experience. Yet we may feel that such a degree of understanding and trust and courage is heroic and not to be counted upon; more often the marriage goes under.

But marriages of this exceptional sort fall outside our consideration here. That people make a failure of their marriage in abnormal conditions is no count against the institution of marriage. The real problem is that so many people make so poor a thing of it in conditions roughly normal. Our concern is with the general average.

(1)

When Mr. Smith marries Miss Jones, it is a common joke that he doesn't know what he is marrying: which usually means that he doesn't know what a temper she has or what she looks like in the early morning. But of almost every man it is true in a profounder sense: he doesn't know what he is marrying, nor does she, because neither knows what a human being is: we are back, in other words, to the theme of this book. Two people have taken each other for better or worse, linked their lives in what might easily prove an intolerable intimacy, and neither knows what the being is to whom he has tied himself so tight. A man had better study what a human being is, because he's marrying one—assuming that merely being one has not been a sufficient stimulus to that study.

In a sense it is a doubling of the strange anomaly that each has been handling himself without knowing what he is, but it is actually far worse. There is a sort of rule-of-thumb knowledge of oneself gained from long experience of being oneself which, though it does not supply for total ignorance of what one is, at least takes some of the chill off it: one has managed to live more or less satisfactorily with oneself, and such dissatisfaction as one feels with one's own performance does not, in most people, turn to resentment. But neither has had any such experience of being the other. A new situation has arisen that the old tried routines cannot cope with: and, in this matter, as in all matters when the routines fail, there must be understanding to cope with the breakdown.

In the close union of marriage all that we have seen in the first section of this book, as to the necessity of knowing and the danger of not knowing what man is, stands clearer than in individual life at the one end or the wider union of Society at the other. Not knowing it can produce more sorrow, knowing it more joy. The pair who have really meditated upon man as a union of matter and spirit, by his spirit immortal and made in God's image, a being for whom Christ died, have made a preparation for marriage for which there is no substitute. If any be disposed to mock at this as doctrinaire and unrealistic, at least let one who thinks he has made a success of marriage mock first. To have failed does not of itself qualify a man to speak as an expert, upon marriage or anything else.

In marriage the view of the essential magnificence of man is at once most urgently needed and most sharply tested. It is harder for the married to go on holding it and grimmer to go on, not holding it. No man is a hero to his valet, says the proverb: and no valet is bound as tight to his master's unposed self as wife and husband to each other's. Distant hills are greenest: in marriage there is no distance at all to create the illusion of any verdure that is not there, or deepen the greenness of any that is. Every man's private face is different from his public face: but the face that the married see is something more private than private—private is too public a word for it. No one sees the husband as the wife sees him—not the husband, certainly; and he has his own unshared view of her for compensation. For being thus unique, the view each has of the other is not necessarily accurate or profound. Each will note the elements in the other that he or she personally responds to most—the response being either of attraction or repulsion: but whereas one may get used to the qualities that attract and take them for granted and cease to respond to them, the irritating more often continue to irritate.

The average issue of all this is hard to set down; indeed it is hard to say if there *is* an average, or if the word average has any meaning, where there is so wide an arc—with something that verges on bliss at one end, and something that skirts the upper edge of the intolerable at the other. But those marriages surely rank high where husband and wife love each other, would feel all lost without each other, are amiably tolerant of each other's faults (and aware of their own); and even in this smaller group the phrase "essential magnificence" applied to either might cause the other to smile. In less happy marriages—which would yet count as successful, which neither party regrets having entered upon—the rejection would be more violent.

Only in the rarest cases will a husband and wife discover each other's magnificence by looking at each other: the way to learn is the way Christian civilization learnt it, by listening to God, who says that it is so. Learn it they must, for it is the truth about themselves, and it is the one sure ground of reverence. It is a main theme of this book that reverence is everywhere essential. In marriage reverence is more important even than love: love will not find its own self without it. Reverence does not mean remoteness or exclude lightheartedness: two who reverence each other can play together. But it does mean a steady awareness in each that the other has a kinship with the eternal.

It is essential that husband and wife reverence each other: it is essential that they reverence the marriage relation. And as the one reverence comes from knowledge of what man is, the other comes from knowledge of what marriage is. In one as in the other, as we have seen, the essential magnificence is as real as any existential degradation there may be. In normal Christian marriage, of course, there is no question of degradation. Yet there may be a failure to realize what marriage essentially is which prevents the marriage reaching its full stature. It may be a failure either to see marriage as a union of personalities, based upon self-giving, or to achieve a bodily union worthy of the total personal relation it is meant to express.

The bodily union may lack perfection either from coldness, where one party goes through the motions mechanically or with positive distaste; or from excess, with one or both concentrated wholly and gluttonously upon the pleasure the body can get out of it and so, with whatever protestation of love, each using the other as a means, a convenience, a thing and not a person. So far as these evils arise from physical or psychological defects they may not be easily curable, or curable at all. But more often they are there because no right view of sex and marriage exists to show any reason for bettering them. Save in the rare instances when everything goes right by a sort of healthy instinct with love blunting all egoisms, understanding is essential. With understanding, most of what is wrong in the physical relation may be made right; with understanding there may be a beginning of the self-giving without which no sexual competence will make a marriage happy, and *with* which marriage may be a thing of excellence even when the sex relation lacks richness. Where the understanding is by both, the marriage will not be wrecked, from within at least. Where one understands and the other does not, it can be tragic—such an infinity of patience and love and wounds endured and no certain success.

(2)

Total self-giving, then, is the key to successful marriage. The self resists, clinging to its autonomy. Love is the key to self-giving. Love can provide a kind of understanding deeper and more dynamic than the intellect at its most powerful will ever know. Love can provide a kind of reverence, too, though this perhaps more before the loved one is possessed—in which case it was reverence for the unknown, a valuable thing but not the real thing: to know and still to revere, that is true reverence. Love can do even that. Love can do every sort of impossibility. The trouble is that love at that intensity is not so very common. Every new pair of lovers feel that they have attained it, like C. S. Calverley's pair—

> We did not love as others do.
> None ever did, that I've heard tell of.*

It has never been as easy as all that, and modern life has made it harder; the waters have been so muddied, love has so much to contend with in the way of psychologies that have half-fouled it for the young before they have grown to feel it. Two or three years of cynicism about sex is no happy preparation for love. Adolescent playing about with sex there has always been: it is a great misfortune, since there is no gift a husband and wife can bring to each other so great as their sexual power in its integrity, not spilled and frittered away in small affairs: it is a great misfortune, but not fatal—not half so deadly as the theoriz-

* Yes, I know that one word in this passage is not the word that Calverley wrote.

ing about sex that the youngest learn now. C. S. Calverley's pair would be harder to find today, when everyone has been taught that love is either chemistry or libido, either way wholly of the body and not unique or especially to be valued. Even through that soggy mass of adverse theory, people do fall in love. And they had better, if they are going to marry. What if they do not?

Love there must be in marriage. But not *necessarily* sexual love. Husband and wife must have at least that love with which Christ said we must love our neighbour. Without that no human relation is possible for them at all. But this sort of love is easier while our neighbour remains our neighbour: it grows harder when he moves in to live with us: even warm friendship finds too close and continuous a proximity trying. Sexual love is different. It is rooted in the will, but it floods the emotional life too, and finds its satisfaction in one particular person of the opposite sex—a satisfaction not to be had only in possessing the other, but equally in giving oneself to be possessed. It is the one love that need not suffer attrition from proximity—even the proximity of the marriage bed. Where there is no sexual love, the sexual act will not easily keep its rightness. For the act is at its healthiest and richest when it expresses a total self-giving; without that it would be performed at best dutifully, at worst either mechanically or too animally, anyhow without resonances in the depths of the personality. And two who are not in love will find it difficult to give themselves thus totally.

This special love, then, is of the first importance. But, for all its power, it has no certainty of permanence. It depends enormously, in its earlier stages at least, upon the feelings: and these go up and down with one's own physical and spiritual state, and with the other's well-or-ill-doing. That is where reverence comes in, which is based upon reason. Married love exists because he is he and she is she. Reverence exists because he and she are human beings, made in God's image, immortal, redeemed by Christ.

Love is based upon the uniqueness of the person loved, reverence upon the common substance of humanity. Love can know disillusion, he is not as she thought him, she had seemed faultless and is not. In the wind of disillusion, love can flicker or blow out altogether. But reverence can know no disillusion: he and she are in their unchanging essence precisely what they were seen to be. That is the sense in which reverence can be more important than love. It gives permanence to marriage. It can even protect love against its own too great volatility.

(3)

A man and a girl may marry, loving each other, and with a clear realization of what man is and what marriage is and what life is and what God is. And their marriage may be a miserably mediocre business all the same. Preparation for marriage is essential. But in another sense you cannot be prepared for it. The newly married have a feeling that what is happening is at once like what they were told and not quite like. A union of personalities is easy enough to theorize about—as swimming is—but the reality can be known only in the experience. Marriage is a sort of sea, with a troubled surface and frightening depths. Swimming lessons on land cannot give you the *feel* of the sea: after however many lessons, the first plunge shows it strange and vast and un-cooperative. In marriage, the new element, of which no thinking of one's own or advice from others can give the feel, is the closeness of life together. And the difficulty is not so much the continuousness of the closeness, day in and day out, night after night for ever, as the quality of the closeness—two beings not simply linked or bound together, but interpenetrating, a sort of permeation—more like air in lungs. It is difficult to say it without making it sound comic. But it is true and it is not comic. Each is the air the other breathes, and the lungs may not, for a long time or perhaps ever, be comfortable with this new air. The bodily penetration is a symbol of the interpenetration of their personalities, and like all good symbols falls far short. So close a union of personalities has two natural results: by their faults, especially by the thrust of self, the two can bruise each other: by their insufficiency they can leave each other unsatisfied.

The defects first. Not much needs to be said of them: they fill the comedies of the world to bursting: it is a poor playwright who cannot be funny about them: he need not invent, for they are there, and they make good comedy—to watch, of course, not to live with. Defects in husband and wife need not be great to be maddening; faults which even in close friendship would not matter at all, matter horribly in marriage. The way one of them sniffs or clears his throat or laughs, a word always mispronounced or a minor grammatical error, can play the devil with the other's nerves, worse indeed than more serious faults. A want of external courtesy can cause more hurt than a really profound want of consideration. A mere disharmony of mood—that one should be gay when the other is depressed—can become a major grievance. And there is the plain human fact of cussedness, being difficult for no reason at all, and sudden gusts of anger and a real desire to hurt and satisfaction in hurting, with love sharpening the satisfaction.

There is no point in listing these things. Most marriages have them and most survive them. A sense of humour helps, though this can be strained to screaming point (and indeed can strain the partner to screaming point, if his own humour be on a different wave-length, or perhaps no wave-length). Common sense helps—only the very immature can tell themselves that somewhere a faultless partner is waiting for them if only they had not stumbled into marriage with one who was imperfect. Most helpful of all, perhaps, is a lively sense of one's own defects, which as we have noted before are not more attractive for being one's own.

But there are graver faults of character—lying still within the area of the average, and not with those abnormal evils mentioned earlier—that show up starkly and press relentlessly on nerves and feelings. It is by these that marriage is really tested. There can be a foul temper, for instance, or suspiciousness or jealousy; one or other may be lazy or spendthrift or "tricky" about money. That these things may not wreck the marriage, there must be unselfishness, sometimes on a heroic scale—which does not mean putting up with anything and everything, but resolutely thrusting one's own feelings aside and doing what is best for the troublesome partner and for the marriage itself. But unselfishness can get a little frayed when it is all on one side, and the faults on the other get no less; indignation—thoroughly justified, be it noted, but all the more corrosive for that—arrives and settles in; and the martyr-complex makes a hell for erring partner and martyr alike, to say nothing of the children.

But one cannot say nothing of the children. A moment can easily arrive when one partner may ask whether the defects of the other call for some more positive action in the children's interests. There is the possibility of self-deception here—a selfish desire to escape, cloaking itself as anxiety for the children's well-being. But the problem is perfectly real. The husband is the head of the family and the woman is the heart. In the human body both organs are marvellously adapted for their functions, and even at that they often function badly. In the family the husband and wife may be extremely, even marvellously, ill-adapted for their very much more delicate functions. The wife may have no heart of her own, or too much heart to the point of sloppiness; the husband no will of his own, or too much to the point of tyranny. In the actual run of life, these things work out well enough, provided that one parent is functioning normally—all, perhaps, except the last: tyranny in the father is hard to cope with and in the nature of the case is not uncommon. Shakespeare gives the clue:

> Man, proud man
> Drest in a little brief authority . . .
> Plays such fantastic tricks before high heaven
> As make the angels weep.

Authority could hardly be littler or briefer than a father's over his family: yet it can go to his head, if he has a weakness that way. All the power he would have gloried in exercising, had life been kind to him—as captain of a warship, say, or ruler of an empire—comes thundering down upon the heads of his family, and the tricks can be very fantastic indeed. A wife may have to consider when she should intervene, and if so how, and whether anyhow intervention is possible. This is not a book of marriage guidance, and I am not drawing up a set of rules by which husband or wife may decide whether or not to separate. I only say that principles as to the nature of man and of marriage should be in their mind when they are making the decision. But experience does seem to suggest two things—separation is so unsatisfactory that it must be a very bad marriage indeed to be worse; and those who have made the sacrifices necessary to hold an unhappy marriage together do not, in the long run, seem to regret it.

I have glanced thus rapidly at the question of how a husband and wife can hurt each other and weaken their marriage, by their faults of character. Of a totally different quality is what I have called insufficiency in the personality.

There is the fact, already referred to, that no human person can meet all another's needs. There are needs that only God can meet. They lie very deep because the first and profoundest fact about man is that he was made for union with God; is hungry, therefore, for union and tormented in its absence. There is the need to adore, for instance, which when not directed to God finds very strange gods indeed; the sense of guilt, when union with God is broken by sin, and the need for cleansing; the need for reassurance in the loneliness and lostness of the creature out of touch with his Creator; the need for revitalization, when the living contact with the Source of all life is snapped. A man need not know what is troubling him to be profoundly troubled: as a man may die of a microbe he has never heard of. If they do not turn to God, a husband and wife will look to each other for the satisfaction of these needs—more especially they will look to the sexual act; they are asking more than the act can give, more than the whole personality can give. Not receiving it, they feel cheated and resentful. Which is one reason why a Christian should not marry an atheist: it is terribly trying to be only a creature, yet expected to meet the needs that only the Creator can meet.

Yet it is not this insufficiency, inseparable from our finitude, that I have in mind here; but a sort of thinness of personality, a negativeness, an absence of qualities that ought to be there—which in extreme cases may be utter mindlessness, flabbiness in the will, dull passions, dull or maybe shrill emotional responses, lack of richness or generosity or any substance. The union of two such personalities is a union of two nullities, like the embrace of two shadows. There is a special awfulness in the marriage of two so mindless that they cannot converse—or even be fruitfully silent: it may be less trying when both are so busy that they meet only at bed and board, but the busyness only marks the vacuum. There are personalities so thin that, without strong religious motives, their marriage cannot last. They have no will to give themselves and almost no selves to give, nothing to hold each other with: fidelity would be a miracle in such marriages. But even short of that degree of nullness, most of us have little enough to offer our partners in marriage. The problem of marriage for the majority is to make something out of a union, if not of two nullities, at least of two insufficiencies.

Surprisingly often it succeeds. There is a power in marriage that tends both to weld and give substance to the personalities. In some mysterious way—mystical might be a better word—there is a communication of substance from one person to the other, and from one sex to the other: each becomes himself plus something of the other. Even a very thin personality begins to take on body when one has to take account of another person; new elements in one's make-up come alive and either unite with elements already in operation or strive with them and stimulate them by strife: so that one is already more of a person. A selfish man who no longer takes his selfishness as sole and unquestioned law of action but is at least troubled by the feeling of duty undone to another is, by that shade, more human than before.

Marriage seems to work magic. But it is not all magic. Husband and wife must work hard at it. If one is making no effort, the other must work twice as hard. Love helps, though it is precisely love that is in danger of losing its élan with so much to depress it; prayer helps tremendously. But, in the purely psychological order, nothing helps so much as the reverence that flows from a right vision of what man is—that this loutish man, this empty-headed woman, is God's image, an immortal spirit, loved by Christ even to the death of the Cross: whatever the surface looks like, this is in the depth of every human being, this in him is what God joined together with this in her. The realization that there is this welding of two into one in the depths of their being, below the level that the eye of the mind can see, is the most powerful incentive to make that union in depth effective through every layer of personality.

This reverence is a safeguard against one of the great dangers of family life—the tendency of one partner to form, or re-form, the other (or for a parent to form the children) in his own image. There is a sort of imperialism to which the self is liable, the desire to impose its own likeness. As we have already seen, one should not lightly try to re-make another: but, if re-making there *must* be, assuredly the only image in which anyone should be re-made is the image of God in which he was made. Children are even more likely to suffer this sort of tyranny than adults. One knows the widowed mother who rules her children with the rod of iron of a dead father's will—"Your father would not have wished it." Of that will she is the sole interpreter, and there is no appeal. Any imposing of oneself on another is a sin against reverence. Reverence is due to all men. It was the Roman poet Juvenal who said that the greatest reverence was due to children. It must have sounded like a paradox to his readers, and possibly a little daring to himself. It is the plain truth; but hard for a parent to see for two reasons: the first is the overwhelming tendency to think one has made them oneself, that they are one's own handiwork; the second is their physical weakness, which makes it tempting to enforce one's own will upon them—the weakness, you observe, may be purely physical, a child of three often has more personality than both parents put together. In *The Way of All Flesh* Samuel Butler has a wonderful phrase about a small boy in nineteenth-century England: "The Catechism was awful. . . . It seemed to him that he had duties towards everybody, lying in wait for him upon every side, but that nobody had any duties toward him." Our Lord provides the element Butler found wanting in the Church Catechism: If anyone scandalize the least of these my little ones, it were better for him if a millstone were hanged about his neck and he were drowned in the depth of the sea."

So far we have been looking at the difficulties that arise

because marriage is the union of two personalities, which have somehow to be harmonized. These difficulties would be tough enough, if there were no sexual element to complicate them. But there is a sexual element. And it complicates them. Sex's head is not always ugly, but it always rears it.

In the making of marriage sexual desire normally plays a part: thus far it has rendered an essential service. But sexual desire is an uneasy servant, not to be relied on simply to serve. It has its own needs, its own urges, its own dreams. And in the marriage it has helped to produce its dreams may dissolve, its needs be unmet, so that its urges take on a new and sometimes frantic urgency. The physical union may be totally unsatisfying, and, if so, bitterly so. This will not necessarily destroy the marriage. Where the union of personalities is richly satisfying, the bodily union gains so much from it that any imperfection at the bodily level is more than compensated. But the perfect spiritual and psychological union is rare, and, short of it, an unsatisfying sexual life can rend a marriage apart: there may be no actual divorce, but the dream of a perfect sexual union will continue to haunt the imagination, so that the meagre reality becomes a torment, and husband or wife or both will go out in pursuit of the dream. This is something quite distinct from mere lust or licentiousness. The "dream" comes from very deep within the personality, and the inspiration is noble in itself and can make for nobility. When two people fall in love, each sees the dream and the aspiration wholly concentrated in the other. It is a woeful thing when marriage shatters them: a woeful thing if the shattering is the fault of either.

I have said that what I have here in mind is not at all

the same thing as lust or licentiousness. But there is lust too: and if only the licentious indulge it, no one at all is exempt from its first stirrings, save in the fruition of a great love. Sexual desire is incalculable. As a mere animal appetite for union with a member of the other sex, any member not actively repulsive, it is calculable enough, and most adults have brought it into some sort of control. What is incalculable is the desire, not for any member of the other sex, but for that particular one. It suddenly flames into life on no known law. But, once it is aflame, the laws of its burning are only too well-known. We know that a man, beginning to desire a woman he ought not to have (because he is married, or she is), can tell himself that it is all quite innocent—he is interested in her for her intellectual or artistic life, or her spiritual problems—and so go on fooling himself right up to the moment of the explosion. At least the high-minded thus fool themselves—the earthier sort know better what they are at. At all times man has that conflict between reason and will of which St. Paul speaks so poignantly, whereby he can see one thing and do another: but in this matter he goes beyond that—sexual desire has a curious power of preventing reason and will from acting at all (as tart apricots, for instance, can prevent the teeth from biting). *Ira furor brevis est,* said Horace. Anger is madness while it lasts. Sexual desire is a sort of somnambulism while it lasts—something in the back of the mind plucking at the sleeve with a reminder of reality as it is, something in the depth of the conscience plucking at the sleeve with a warning to stand and go no further: but mind and will not gripping, the dream in full possession. Sexual desire, one says again, is incalculable and (save about the precise object of desire) uncalculating.

It can fix itself anywhere: can will incompatibles: can will what it does not want—if will be the word for it. Desire for one woman may momentarily eclipse love for another, and the eclipsed love can outlast the desire, so that a moment comes when the love is in full possession again, and the dead desire seems mere emptiness and degradation.

Everyone knows all this, and knowing it does not cure it. But a serious effort to realize it is not waste, for all that. For in the first place it is a reminder that all carry their treasure in earthen vessels, even young lovers newly married, who feel exultantly that they and their love are beyond the reach of mortal accident, even the middle-aged long-married, who feel that these are fires that will never flame again. It can save them all from over-testing their supposed strength: the danger is less for the man who knows it can happen to him. And in the second place it shows where the precautions must be taken and what counter-action is profitable. The temptations of this sort that come to people satisfyingly in love are fewer and more manageable: where a husband and wife meet each other's psychological and physical needs, the odds against the stranger are very high. There is still a magic of the moon, but the daylight magic of the sun is greater. Only when the daylight magic has faded, when the sensed daylight has grown less, when the whole of life together has become a routine, even if a pleasant routine—then is the dangerous moment.

Yet, when all is said, whether the level of conjugal vitality be high or low, the most powerful safeguard against infidelity, in the bodily act or only in the mind, is that clear view of man and of marriage which at every point we have seen as fundamental. The moral law—known not only as a set of prohibitions, but as the expression of the way of life seen as best for us by a loving Creator—can give a strength and steadiness to mind and will, and even limit the field of temptation. There is an extraordinary psychological force in regarding certain things as out of the question. In all ages, men and women have been born, one presumes, with homosexual tendencies: but in healthier ages homosexuality was felt to be altogether unthinkable, and the tendencies therefore came to nothing: in our own society, which regards homosexuality as unusual but an interesting variant of the normal all the same, the temptation to let the tendencies have their way can prove irresistible. So with adultery. A social attitude that regards it as impossible does at least make it improbable. We can no longer rely on a general consensus of opinion that any sort of sexual deviation is out of the question. But individual men and women can provide the same sort of psychological strengthening for themselves, by so studying and meditating upon the nature of man and the law of God that what these require becomes a vital part of the world they are mentally living in.

To many all that we have been saying will seem Utopian. The sex instinct seems so powerful that to expect the generality of men to control it is like urging tranquillity upon a man with St. Vitus's dance. But this is to underrate the generality of men. There is a vast store of moral health which does not normally show very spectacularly in moral action, perhaps, but shows unmistakably in other ways—especially in two ways—negatively in a total inability to find happiness in self-indulgence, positively in an astounding readiness for sacrifice for a cause seen as good. Exceptional men will die as martyrs to science: the most ordinary man will die helping the stricken in an epidemic or in war for their country. Men will sacrifice themselves for any ideal that they value. The integrity of marriage does not seem to them such an ideal. Why should it? Who has ever shown them the enormous human interests involved in it? At any rate we can say of marriage what we have already seen true of social relations in general, that we are not entitled to say men will make no sacrifice for the ideal, until we have done something to show them why it *is* the ideal.

SOCIETY AND STATE

11

Society and the Nature of Man

JUST AS THE individual cannot satisfy his own needs or express his own powers himself, but requires the family, so families cannot by themselves satisfy all the needs of their members or give scope for the development of all the powers of their members.

They cannot satisfy all man's *needs*. A man, for example, can learn a great deal in the family, and some of this he could not learn anywhere else. But there is a vast mass of truth, nourishing to the intellect and essential if it is to reach the fulness of its powers, which the family cannot teach him. He must learn it outside. So likewise with his material needs: he needs food and drink and clothing and housing far beyond the powers of a single family to provide.

As with man's needs, so with his *powers*. He has that in him to communicate—truth to teach, songs to sing—which cannot stay within the four walls of the family; there is the world to be explored, nature to be studied and brought into man's further service.

For this wider satisfaction and development, a larger group is needed. Families must be united in Society. A man might, of course, live a diminished life of body and mind wholly within his family circle, but there is one overwhelming need which could not be met at all, the need for protection. Against the violence of individuals, men *must* group themselves, or one by one they will perish.

(1)

From this first quick glance two things should be clear: first, that man cannot do without Society, Society is more or less forced upon him; but second, that Society is not just a piece of mechanism—any more than Marriage is—a clever dodge thought up by Nature in the interests of the race, with the individual man constrained, or tricked, into it at whatever cost to his own personality. Society, like Marriage, is forced upon man only in the sense that his nature is forced upon him; and, like Marriage, it brings an enrichment to his own personality. Society is not simply a necessary evil, to be put up with, as Belloc says children should

> . . . always keep a-hold of nurse
> For fear of finding something worse.

Society is a positive good. Only in it can man be fully himself. We have already noted the first instinctive movement of man outward to his fellows, the mere desire to be with them, the awfulness of solitude too long continued. Then from being with them, powers stir into life, powers to serve and be served, such a rich profusion of powers up to the fulness of co-operation in a developed social order. Nor have we any reason to think that the social element in man's nature has yet revealed all its possibilities. Those who do not exercise their full activity in Society, who live their lives outside the main stream of Society's life, are lessened as men. There are selfish men, for instance, to whom the social order is only a convenience enabling them to concentrate in security upon their own business or pleasure, indolent men who fear to plunge into a stream so turbulent. The result is always the same—needs unnourished, powers left to atrophy, and the ignobility of the refusal to make all worse.

It may be by exclusion, not by refusal, that men are outside the fulness of Society. The Catholics in England, between the Reformation and Catholic Emancipation, were thus excluded, permitted barely to live upon the fringe of society: they suffered in a noble cause, but they did suffer, not only materially but psychologically and spiritually, the contribution to human and political life that they had it in them to make not made, the strength that flows from recognition and fellowship not flowing for them. That England lost more by excluding them than the Catholics by being excluded does not make their loss less real. They were forced to seek in the Church the compensation for what Society denied them. And indeed, by the accident of history, this remains a tendency of English-speaking Catholics everywhere. In Ireland, even more than in England—and in the new worlds growing from both, America, for instance, and Australia—they were too long excluded from full recognition as members of Society and full participation in its life; they existed on sufferance, and functioned socially hardly at all. Disowned by their natural Society, they were driven more and more to think of, and live in, the Church as their only *patria;* and the habit lingers.

It is not a good habit. The Church is a more perfect

society, meeting deeper needs more richly, more of a community, uniting its members more intimately, than any purely human organization. But life in the super-natural society was never meant as a *substitute* for life in the natural society. It was never meant as a substitute, and is not in fact a substitute. The Church is a society of too special a sort, its structure and functions created by God not developed by its members, not made by them in the first place nor alterable by them; its members do not make the same *sort* of contribution to the super-natural society as to the natural, do not exercise their powers in it or exert their influence upon it in the same way, they belong to it but they do not feel that it is their property as civil society is, it is not theirs to re-make if they will—a citizen could take action against a bad king, for instance, that a Catholic could not take against a bad Pope; and though their profoundest needs are met in it, there are all sorts of other needs, profound too and related to the full development of their manhood, which it was not created to meet. The Church is no more a substitute for civil Society than for the family.

Society, then, exists to answer certain demands of man's nature—man cannot attain his full development as a man, save by co-operation with masses of his fellows. So that it, too, like the family, is grounded in man's nature. Any given arrangement of Society may be artificial, but Society itself is natural. Thus Society too has rights—all the rights required to perform its essential service to man—and these also are grounded in man's nature. But the ways in which men have to work together for the good of all are extraordinarily complex: such a complexity, with human minds and human wills and human passions and emotions to complicate it further, would be sheer chaos, if it were not brought into order by authority, and authority clothed with power.

For the order that authority exists to bring into being will not please everyone—partly because men will differ in judgment as to its wisdom, but still more because it must very often impinge upon self-interest. Society is for the good of all, the Common Good. But, things being as they are, the Common Good is not likely to be the same as the fullest possible good that each man desires for himself. The Common Good may require that Society be protected against the violence of men or the violence of nature, so that some will be called upon to risk their lives. Short of that, the Common Good may require many things against which self-will rebels—a distribution, for instance, of the material resources of Society, so that some men will have less than by their own efforts they could seize, in order that others may not go destitute; a checking of the natural instinct to seize what is one's own by force and a submission of one's claim to a tribunal; even the acceptance of a decision that seems unjust rather than disturb the order so essential to the well-being of all.

All this means that Society cannot exist unless the authority that gives orders is able to enforce them. Authority clothed with power is thus required by the nature of man, so that it, too, is natural. Authority is *not* conferred upon Society by its members. Since social authority is a demand of man's nature, men no more confer authority upon Society than they confer their nature upon themselves. They are free to decide how this authority shall be exercised—for example by republic or monarchy or what you will. But the authority thus exercised is not created by them. The power that gave man his nature gives Society its authority. Authority is God-given.

We have arrived at this truth simply by looking at the nature of man. We find it also in the law of God. Christ Our Lord uttered it for us in one sentence—"Render to Caesar the things that are Caesar's, and to God the things that are God's."

St. Peter and St. Paul each writes his own commentary upon the phrase.

St. Peter writes (I Peter ii. 13), "For love of the Lord, bow to every kind of human authority; to the king, who enjoys the chief power, and to the magistrates who hold his commission to punish criminals and encourage honest men. . . . Give all men their due; to the brethren, your love; to God, your reverence; to the king, due honour."

St. Paul writes (Rom. xiii. 1–7), "Every soul must be submissive to its lawful superiors; authority comes from God only, and all authorities that hold sway are of His ordinance. Thus the man who opposes authority is a rebel against the ordinance of God, and rebels secure their own condemnation. A good conscience has no need to go in fear of the magistrate, as a bad conscience does. If you would be free from the fear of authority, do right, and you shall win its approval; the magistrate is God's minister working for your good. Only if you do wrong need you be afraid; it is not for nothing that he bears the sword; he is God's minister still, to inflict punishments on the wrongdoer."

The fact that the king reigning when they wrote was Nero, who executed them both, adds a kind of piquancy to their teaching. But it makes no difference to us in reading it, and would have made none to them: they probably expected it, in any event. The principles stand. Christ certainly, with His "Render to Caesar," knew very well what Caesar was within a few days to render to Him. In fact He made that very rendering an occasion to say it again; for in the trial that brought Him to death He said to Caesar's magistrate, Pilate, "You would not have any power against me, unless it were given you from above."

We have it then on Christ's word that certain things are Caesar's and must be rendered to him; not to render them is to disobey Christ. Because Christ is God, it follows that Caesar's authority has divine ratification, is of divine right. The phrase must not be misunderstood. Every man has a divine right to his life, but this does not mean that he is responsible to no one but God for the way he uses his life. Caesar's authority is God-given, but that does not mean that he is responsible only to God for the use he makes of it. Note also that his authority does not depend upon his being sinless—Nero was notably not—nor upon his being infallibly right, but only upon his being the rightful authority, acting in his proper sphere. I have already quoted the great tribute paid by the first Pope to Caesar. Eighteen hundred years later Peter's successor then reigning, Leo XIII, wrote in the Encyclical *Immortale Dei,* "Hallowed in the minds of Christians is the very idea of public authority, in which they recognize some likeness and symbol of the Divine Majesty, even when it is exercised by one unworthy."

Historically there have been two main types of social authority—the one patriarchal, authoritarian, regal, despotic, the other tribal, popular and elective. One tends to think of Caesar as symbol of the first, not the second. But from

Christ's use of the word, and from the Church's continuing commentary upon the text, Caesar has come to stand for the civil authority, whatever the form of government may be, and in the rest of this book I shall use the word in that sense. If we think of the State as being Society organized for the Common Good, clothed with authority and with the right to exercise force where its authority is resisted, then Caesar is the head of the State. Caesar thus has no rights that Society has not got. The purpose of Society is simply to act that part in the proper development of life upon earth which neither the individual nor the family can act in isolation. Any action by Caesar that hinders the development of man, that makes a man less of a man, is simply monstrous, a contradiction of the function which is the sole foundation for his authority. Yet the Common Good, as we have noted, may mean very considerable sacrifices of individual interests. Caesar—I am using the word for *the man or combination of men in whom civil authority is vested*—has to hold a most delicate and difficult balance. It is not surprising that he seldom holds it perfectly.

(2)

There is another difficult and delicate balance to be held. Caesar is pre-eminent in authority, for his alone is the official function of assuring the Common Good. He is pre-eminent in power, and may not be lightly, or for the most part even safely, resisted. Unless he is a man of singular intellectual clarity he can hardly help feeling that he is a superior being, and that the generality of men exist for his service. But the State—and Caesar therefore as its head—exists for man, not man for the State. The State, as this special organization of Society for the Common Good, not only exists to serve men, but in its own nature is a lesser being than the humblest of its members. For of itself, it has no consciousness and no will, it has nothing but what individual men bring to it. And it is a creature of time, and men are not. The State as such is concerned with the life of man upon this earth, but it will be healthy only if it realizes that this is not the whole of man's life. Its job is not to lead men to heaven, of course, but to make the best arrangement of the earthly affairs of beings whose goal is heaven. It keeps the proportions right to realize that the State will one day end and that no one of its members will. If man is not known to be immortal, then he is seen, and sees himself, only as a replaceable spare part in a machine that looks more eternal than he. But knowing his immortality, the poorest slave can say to the mightiest empire "I will outlive you." He will outlive Caesar, too, *as* Caesar. The man who happens to be Caesar will survive like the slave, in hell, maybe—even if in heaven, without his earthly authority. That is why no man can be lord of another, save for certain specified social purposes. But it is hard for Caesar always to remember this, with all men calling him Lord, hard indeed to remember that he is only a convenience, in the strictest sense *servus servorum Dei,* a servant of men, who are servants of God.

But if Caesar should remember his lowliness as a man, his subjects should see his grandeur in the scheme of their lives. Society is not a mere external organization, but an organic union with other images of God. As we have seen, it is not some clever scheme that nature has imposed or man thought up, but the very condition of his own fulness of human development. The truth is that there must be reverence flowing both ways between Caesar and his subjects, and there is ill-health in a Society that lacks it. Reverence we have seen as the essential law of all human relationships. Without reverence, Society can be at best only mechanism, at worst a horrid rat-race,

> Where he shall take who has the power
> And he shall keep who can.

Caesar must reverence his subjects, both as men, and as men whom it is his function to serve. The subjects must reverence Caesar, both as a man, and as their ruler. It is very bad for Society when Caesar is not reverenced, cynicism about Caesar corrodes the whole of the shared life of men.

In these converging duties of reverence, it is hard to say which has the tougher task.

How is Caesar to reverence his subjects? He sees their faults as no one else can, for he can distribute benefits, and greed is one of the commonest and least attractive of human qualities. The abiding temptation for Caesar is contempt for men: it was a very able Caesar indeed—Sir Robert Walpole, Prime Minister of England in the eighteenth century—who said "Every man has his price." In any form of government, men will fawn upon Caesar in the hope of advantage, and so make it difficult for him to preserve his sense of reverence for man. In an autocracy, a further difficulty arises. Caesar can be deceived by his own trappings—indeed the one argument against rich vestments is that they so easily mislead the wearer into thinking he is somebody.

And how shall his subjects reverence Caesar? They can see how necessary his function is, and so are in the way to reverencing his office. But, at any rate in a modern State, they cannot help seeing the man, the man existential, and it is hard to go on revering the office while despising the holder. Because this is so, it is better to keep a tight rein upon one's judgment of the personal character of the ruler, since all must suffer as irreverence for him corrodes reverence for his office. This particular reverence is probably harder in a democracy, because the citizens have the continuing awareness that they put Caesar into office, and could put him out again, so that they regard him simply as their employee, a relationship in which reverence is by no means automatic. And Caesar likewise is aware that popular will may hurl him from his eminence, and unless he be a man of notable character he will be tempted to forfeit reverence further by a good deal of fawning of his own.

Where reverence is lacking you get cynicism and the sort of realism discussed in Chapter 5. Caesar perfects himself in the art of handling the citizens to the end that he may remain Caesar: and the citizens develop all the arts whereby every man tries to protect himself, against unjust exactions first, and soon against any demands at all. Reverence is gone: duty is gone: all is reduced to a contest of cunnings, a pitting of wits, a degradation of society in which the individual is not likely to remain undegraded.

(3)

Civil authority is from God; so that the laws of a State are binding in conscience, binding, as a Catholic would say, under sin. In his standard work *Moral and Pastoral Theology* (vol. ii, p. 88), Father Henry Davis, S.J., writes:

> The civil authority derives its power of government—legislative, coercive, vindictive, from God. It does not concern us to define or prove any theory as to the origin of civil authority: it is certain and admitted by all Catholic teachers that the people cannot capriciously change their polity, refuse to obey just laws, or induce others to disobey them, or raise rebellion or sedition against an authority that has been legitimately constituted. When a ruler has been legitimately designated, then he becomes, by the law of nature, the supreme civil authority, and derives his power ultimately from God. He can, therefore, exact obedience that binds under sin.

To be thus binding, laws have not to be infallibly right or wise, any more than Caesar himself has to be. I may think a given law not only not the best in the circumstances but plainly foolish or actually harmful, yet my obligation is to obey. The reason is plain enough. If laws were obeyed only by the citizens who approved of them, civil society would be at an end. Caesar cannot be all-wise or all-good, and some of his laws will be unsound. But the citizens are not perfect either, intellectually or morally; in a general way they are no wiser or better than Caesar or as well-informed, so that a given man's judgment of the soundness of this or that law is not necessarily right; not only that, but the citizens are so various that approval and disapproval would differ from one man to the next, some would choose to disobey this law and some that; so that laws would cease to be laws and become suggestions offered by Caesar or hints he drops; you would no longer have a civil society but chaos. And even with very imperfect laws, society is better than chaos, as it is better to live in a draughty house than to live in a tree.

Laws then must not be regarded as a set of obstacles to be crashed through or hurdled or evaded. They must be respected as a condition of the vital functioning of Society. They must be respected indeed as a condition of freedom, for the only alternative to the rule of law is the tyranny of the strongest. Within the rule of law there is, of course, another danger, the dominance of the cunning. Men study the law to see how they can at once observe it and subvert it: which is only another form of disrespect for law. And in societies where strong men or cunning men, or a combination of strong men and cunning men, have been too long in control, the laws themselves will be used for oppression, and it is hard for men who have known law only as oppression to respect it. Yet it remains the truth that a healthy society will not exist where law is not respected.

There is a special difficulty here in a democracy, or rather two difficulties, related to the problem already mentioned of respect for Caesar himself. The first is that we put the lawmakers in, so that we feel we made the laws ourselves; we can throw them out, so that we feel that the laws depend on our agreement. Respect for law is not easy for men who feel that the law is their creature. The second is that contest for high office is fierce: whoever wins enters upon office muddied with the mud thrown at him, muddied quite likely with the mud he has thrown, anyhow resented by nearly half of the citizens: and in office he is still resented and slandered: it is hard to treat the laws he makes as objects of reverence. Distinctions have to be held clear which to tired minds or hurried minds are by no means clear. As to the second difficulty: laws may be passed by men we despise, but they come to us with all the authority of Society, for by these men Society has chosen that its affairs shall be conducted. And as to the first: the making of the law may depend upon our consent; but while it exists it binds us all the same. There is something here that faintly resembles what happens in marriage. A man is free to marry or not to marry; the making of the marriage depends upon his consent; but while it exists it binds him. The difference is, of course, that it exists till his death or his partner's: whereas between citizens and their laws divorce is always possible: which does not make laws any easier to respect.

Laws are laws, whether they are wise or unwise. But not every ordinance issued even by a rightful authority is necessarily a law. If it contradicts the law of God or the nature of man, it is not a law at all, but a monstrosity, an anti-law, and not binding. If it contradicts God's law, it must not be obeyed. If it contradicts man's nature, the question will arise whether the contradiction is serious enough to justify resistance, considering that Society is itself a need of man's nature and resistance to law weakens Society. Whatever the decision may be, it remains true that no ordinance is law that is out of harmony with the law of God and the nature of man.

It is important that Caesar and citizens should be *agreed* about what man is and what God wills for him, otherwise there is no unity between them as to man's rights and how he should be treated, but only conflict and no way of settling it, not really a social order at all but half-chaos, with governors grabbing power because they think they can, and the governed resisting when the pressure gets too painful. It is still more important that Caesar and citizens should be *right* about both: for they constitute the laws of Reality, and no amount of agreement to collide with the laws of Reality will make the collision anything but destructive.

(4)

In this first general consideration of man in society one question remains to be mentioned. We have seen that God gives authority to Society, and that Society decides through what organs—king or parliament, autocracy, oligarchy, democracy—the authority shall be exercised. Most of the world's debate is upon this second matter, whether authority in the State is best exercised by this form of government or that. It is an important question, but not the most important. Not "Who shall exercise the power?" but "How much power?" is the essential question. God has given authority to Society; but what is its field? What are its limits?

At the moment the sky is filled with the clang of battle between Totalitarianism and Democracy. In fact there is no necessary opposition between them. They are answers to two different questions.

Totalitarianism is an answer to the question "What things are Caesar's?"—the answer it gives being that all things whatsoever are Caesar's, that the State's right of control is unlimited, that the citizen has no rights against the State, no part of life that is simply his own.

Democracy is an answer to the question "Who is

Caesar?"—the answer it gives being that Caesar is whomever the People elects.

Obviously there is no necessary opposition between them. One State might easily give both answers. It might decide that authority resides in the People, and that the People elects its government and can change its government. And it might also decide that there is no limit to the People's control, through that elected and dismissible government, over the life of the individual, that, for what is conceived to be the good of the totality, the individual may be totally regimented. There is no paradox here, no improbability even. A government which can claim to be doing what the majority of the people think best can interfere in the life of citizens as the most absolute tyrant could not: it was not an autocrat who in this century imposed Prohibition upon a great people: no autocrat would have dared. In fact control by government is spreading so fast in the democracies that the distinction already noted between the two main types of social authority has less meaning than of old, and Caesar is as good a symbol for one as for the other.

I have said that the question "How much power?" is far more important than the question who exercises it. This the Catholic Church has always seen. Between forms of government—dictatorship, monarchy, republic—she is neutral; under any of them God can be obeyed and man be man. But as to the extent of power, which is the reality of government, she cannot possibly be neutral. For herself as for the citizen it is the question that really matters. It is a calamity that we should be so urgent about the forms, so little concerned about the reality.

12

Social Fact and Political Order

(1)

WE HAVE already seen the distinction between Society and State. The State is Society as organized, exercising authority, and wielding power. Society is larger than the State: for though both are made up of the same people Society contains these people in wider interests. The unit of Society is a man, of the State a citizen: and a man is more than a citizen. Every man *is* a citizen, but not only a citizen. It is not the citizen who embraces his wife and begets his children, but the man: it is the man who plays his games and dreams his dreams, paints his pictures, talks all night with his friends, gazes at the moon and curses the mosquitoes: the man who worships his God and serves Him well or ill. Shakespeare was a citizen: but that was not his greatest excellence or his greatest usefulness to Society. Because Society and State are made up of the same individuals, there will be overlapping between the Social Order and the Political. But the two orders must not be confused.

In Society, a man is doing as he chooses. In the State a citizen is doing as he is told: what he is told may very well be what he would in any event choose, but, whether or no, he must do it or take the consequences. The State, of course, is not only (as Marx says) the organ of force, but of authority and order and the common good. The force is no more than a regrettable necessity: but it *is* regrettable and it is so evidently there.

Put all these considerations together and one sees why Society—we call it our country—stirs emotions so much richer and deeper. When a man thinks of the State, he thinks of the politician, the bureaucrat, the policeman, the tax-collector. When he thinks of his Country, there are no such clearly defined and universal images. In England the head of Society is the King; he is the head of the State, too, but that is not how men think of him. In the United States, if a stranger may be allowed a guess, the President is thought of as the head of the State, but hardly of the Country. It may be that the profound psychological and emotional values attaching to the King of England attach to the Flag of America. At any rate, one country sings "God Save the King" and the other "The Star-Spangled Banner": there is no national hymn about Parliament or Congress: no nation-wide song even, perhaps no song at all. It may not be fanciful, indeed, to think of the characteristic figure in the State as the maker of laws, in Society, the Country, as the maker of songs. Fletcher of Saltoun's friend was right who said he did not care who made a nation's laws, if he might be allowed to make its ballads. The lawmaker has one unanswerable argument, of course. He can stop the song in the singer's throat: for his hands are strong enough. But Society will be the poorer for it, and in the end the lawmaker will be the weaker. For vitality flows from Society to the State, and not the other way.

You cannot codify all this. It is overpoweringly felt, but much of it lies deeper than words. Which is why the patriot does not shine in argument with the cynic. He cannot say what it is that he loves. So much of it is right inside him. If you ask him, his thought flies perhaps to some piece of scenery—as Hilaire Belloc's to Sussex—in which the whole seems somehow implicated, or to some moment of his boyhood not statably significant but richly charged with contentment and certitude. Things of this sort cannot be said lucidly. But no one should smile at his stammering: we should distrust love that is too glib in statement, whether love of woman or love of country. A man loves a woman because he is he and she is she, and it is hard to expound those two truths at length, convincingly. So with a man's love for his country. In his own country a man feels at home, at ease; he is himself there, nourished, warmed (even when physically undernourished and unwarmed). Something in his soul, something in his blood and bones, responds to something in his Country: the most obvious evils he will blame upon the State, and even those which are clearly in Society itself do not easily kill love. Deep calls to deep. The cynic does not feel it, either because he has not got a deep or because he has rationalized himself out of contact with it. The love may be stammering, but it is love. A man *will* lay down his life for his country, and he would still find it hard to express, in a manner luminous to the cynic, what he is dying for—not parliament or congress certainly—or why it is *dulce et decorum,* a joy and a glory, to do it. Death for one's country is rather a special sort of death; most men do not die that way. But if love of country comes to a high intensity only in such moments and in normal times is not much adverted to, it has a day-by-day level all the same. Love of country need not be continuously passionate to be real.

This is Patriotism and a virtue. It has nothing to do with Nationalism, which is a great evil. Love of one's own land no more implies despising other lands than love of one's own mother implies despising other mothers. Patriotism, in fact, bears somewhat the same relation to Nationalism as family affection to snobbery. Patriotism, like family affection, is an expression of love, Nationalism, like snobbery, is an extension of egoism. Not only that. The Patriot, regarding love of country as normal, is happiest with foreigners who love their own country as he loves his. The Nationalist has no corresponding feeling. Indeed he has only a sketchy sort of love even for his own Country. When he says "My country" the emphasis is so much on the "My." The mark of the Nationalist is hatred: he almost invariably hates some other country more than he loves his own; he takes the intensity of his hatred as a measure of his love, and another's lack of that hatred as a lack of love, so that he will rend one of his own countrymen for not hating enough. This is a great evil, but the cure for it is not to stop loving one's own country. Love of family can be perverted into snobbery, love of woman into promiscuity. But the cure for snobbery is not that men should cease to love their kin, or for promiscuity that men should cease to love women. Like these, Nationalism is a perversion of love, and the cure is not to abandon love but to rectify it, purify it.

It is a delusion to think that men will love mankind more if they love their countrymen less. Indeed the internationalists one meets, who have risen beyond love of country, seem to have shed a good deal of love in the process; they do not strike one as especially loving, often enough one gets the impression that they are more devoted to mankind than to men, and more devoted to their system than to mankind. By nature love is felt more intensely at the centre—most intensely for those close to us, less intensely as we move outwards. But the greater the love at the centre, the greater the radiation. Man has one will to love with, and one loving-power: and his loving-power grows by loving and is lessened by ceasing to love. The man who lacks love for his country is a diminished man: not so diminished as if he lacked love for his family, but there is less to him, all the same. A man need not be born there to feel it; he may have come from another country and adopt this one by an act of his will: he can genuinely love his chosen country—but not if its own children do not. The country, if one there be, which does not inspire love is a diminished country, and, however well-organized the State, it is not stable. As in marriage, stability does not rest upon concrete foundations but on a thing so intangible as love, the one thing stronger than death.

Caesar's own stability depends upon his success in getting this love, which is not love *of* him, to run *for* him—men feeling that the country is in good hands. This does not mean simply that the government is efficient; but that it is spiritually and psychologically in tune with its people. It is surprising what the citizens will put up with from a Caesar they feel to be their own sort of man, with their own scale of values and their own view of how life should be ordered: England recently has been through every sort of privation, but the supporters of the Labour Party were prepared to excuse everything, because they felt the government was their own. Every sane Caesar wants thus to be loved, not by half of the citizens, but by the people as a whole. Otherwise he has only superior force or fraud to rely on. This is the organic sense in which government is by consent of the governed.

(2)

That Caesar should want love of country to run for him is only an illustration of the wider truth that *the Political Order should grow out of the Social Fact,* which simply means that a country should be governed in the way it suits this mass of men to be governed, not the way some doctrinaire thinks they should. Today this cardinal principle is very much in eclipse. It has three plain consequences, and the tendency to ignore these is a special weakness—the ignoring of two of them almost ruling vices—of our age.

The first consequence is that *where there is no Social Fact you cannot have a Political Order.* There is a tremendous desire to create a World Political Organization, a World Federation, some sort of World State. It is a desire more honourable than the folly of the doctrinaire —more honourable, for it comes not from a foolish desire to re-make other peoples in one's own image, but from a desperate effort to save the world from what looks like certain catastrophe. The error lies in the idea that a Political Order can be brought into being, and kept in health, while not growing out of an already existent Social Fact. The men of a given country are aware of their oneness in Society and can be organized therefore into a State. They share a strong feeling for their country, they have the similarity of outlook that comes from a shared past, from speaking the same language, from living under the same laws, reading the same books, singing the same songs; in a general way they agree about how men should be treated and life conducted, which is one of the essential matters in the practical order. So far there exists no such feeling for the world or for mankind as a whole; men have no such devotion to the planet as to their country; no such sense of oneness with the human race as a whole, no consciousness of a shared past or pride in the same heroic dead, but different laws, books, songs and a thousand languages. Worst of all, they have not even a common view of how men should be treated, still less how women should be treated or children. There is in this sense no World Social Fact to serve as a foundation for a World Political Order. Clearly those who propose the Political Order hope that it will produce the Social: which is very much like hoping that if you insert the tree it will produce the soil.

A World Political Order is not at this moment possible. But two less ambitious aims we might have. The first is to set up a machinery for keeping the peace, which will fall short of a Political Order but might achieve its immediate object: it may not work, but there is no folly in making the effort. The second is to see if some sort of Political Order be possible not for the whole world, but for such larger aggregations—the Western World, for example—as seem to have a sufficiency of spiritual and psychological values, outlooks and memories in common.

The second consequence of our general principle is that *there is no universally best Political Order*. That Political

Order is best which best suits the Social Fact. A great evil of our day is such a devotion to the Political Order of one's own country that one tries to impose it upon others. Democracy of the ballot-box sort, for example, suits our country. We are—not exactly shocked, not exactly horrified, but let us say distressed, to find a country that is not, at any rate in this sense, or perhaps in any sense, democratic. Our fingers are itching to give them a parliament and universal suffrage and a secret ballot. It is hard to disentangle all the strands of unawareness woven together to make this folly. There is unawareness of the long, slow development by which we ourselves arrived at it: we did not begin with it, it was not imposed upon us, we grew that way through centuries. Out of our own special psychological, social, economic attitudes and needs—rooted in the sort of people our fathers were and the situation in which they found themselves, and changing under the hammering of events—this way of government slowly emerged as the way for us. Of the same sort as this first unawareness is the second—that other people had different fathers in different situations, and different events to hammer them into different attitudes and needs; so that what suits the very special people we are may not suit the very special people they are, they may not be able to make it work, they may not even like it. And there is a third unawareness that in the life of our own Society is even more serious—a failure to realize that Democracy is a high and difficult enterprise. It is an insult to Democracy to think you have but to instal a ballot-box: it calls for a special sort of understanding, education and character: and without these the machinery of Democracy will be functioning in a vacuum and soon will not be functioning at all.

I have said that the desire to impose one's own system upon another country is an evil of our age; related to it, but more monstrous, is an evil that our age seems to have invented, the desire to impose another country's system upon one's own. While Hitler lived, there were Fascists in every country, and some of them believed that their own country would be happier and better under German rule. Communists did not wait for Hitler's coming, or cease with his going, to plan for the imposition of the Russian system—the imposition in fact of Russia—upon their country. There has never been in the world so strange a thing (though in the French Revolution time there was a foreshadowing of it). In every country are men who would hand over their country to another, and that other a country which the vast majority of them have never seen and will never see—and these not simply bad men on the make, but honourable men, idealists. Only a very profound discontent with life in their own Society could produce so naive a belief in the greenness of that distant, invisible hill. The discontent can be noble enough in its origin; but it is perverted in its issue. There may be clamourous evils in the political order, deep-lying corruption in the social order. A given Communist, or a given Fascist, might feel that the only way of health for his country lay in passing under the dominion of that idealized other, so that what looked like treason would be true patriotism. Their conscience is not for us to judge, but their folly is plain for anyone to see.

It is the folly we have already seen working the other way, the idea that a Political Order can be imposed on a Social, whereas it must grow out of it. However bad a country may be in creating its own social order, any other country, meddling, will be worse. You can, if you are strong enough, ignore the Social Fact and impose any Political System you please, and if you are strong enough you can maintain it. But it will not be a Political *Order,* it will not be a natural growth. And it will either die quickly or it will devitalize the Society subjected to it.

The third consequence is that *the Political Order should keep its place as the outgrowth of the Social and not try to re-shape the Social to its own taste.* The tendency everywhere is to make the Political Order and the Social identical—the two are becoming one, and the one is the Political. The State is spreading over into Society, establishing the scale of values by which Society should live, taking over functions which belong to man's personality. Education is an instance, which goes to the very shaping of men. Educators are increasingly functionaries of the State rather than of Society, and are talking of "the kind of citizens the State wants" when in the right order we should be striving for the kind of State the citizens want. What all this means is that the order of Compulsion is spreading into the field of Freedom; as one grows the other must shrink. This spread is the main social and political fact of the day. It is essential that we understand it.

Why is it happening? In the totalitarian states it comes from the ruling doctrine, that man has no meaning save as a cog in the collective machine: progress lies in making the collective more and the cog less. In the democracies it comes from no such conscious motive, but merely by a sort of drift under the pressure of the appalling complexity of modern society. Those in authority feel that it simplifies their job if they decide more and more things themselves, instead of leaving them to the frequently erratic, and invariably various, decision that each man makes for himself. The same desire to simplify works for Nationalization—with the poor applauding: property has always been used to exploit them, and, as it passes from private hands, the threat seems to disappear. But it does not disappear. It accompanies the property, giving the State the economic control of men's lives, which the rich used to have, to add to the political control it already has by nature. Concentration of property, whether in the hands of the rich or of the State, is always a threat to liberty, but greater in the hands of the State. When one same authority not only rules us all but also employs us all, we are wholly helpless. We deceive ourselves if we think it safe for the State to own everything, provided everybody owns the State. One-one hundred and forty millionth part of the ownership of our Country, giving us a theoretical right to one-one hundred and forty millionth share in the decisions the State makes about our personal lives, is not at all the same thing as liberty.

I have spoken of all this movement as a matter of doctrine in one set of countries, of drift in another. But, doctrine or drift, underlying it is something in the very nature of power. The State has power, and it is a law of nature that power tends to spread—not because it is tyrannical, or imperialistic, or particularly evil, but simply because it is power—it spreads like ink in blotting-paper. There are all sorts of reasons for this, but one, I think, is particularly in evidence today. As power grows, it grows fearful: very much as the miser grows fearful, the more his money mounts. There is a high incidence of insanity among tyrants, and it is always of the same sort—fear, suspiciousness: other men need not be powerful to be feared as rivals, they need only be other: they must either be destroyed or somehow absorbed into, made part of, the tyrant. Power is jealous; and the immense effort to absorb the Social Order into the Political certainly involves a desire to win for the rulers of the State the emotional values that go with the Country. It is a profound error. Those emotional values arise precisely from freedom, responsibility, all the things that the order of compulsion must diminish; they grow in a strongly personal Social Order and pour their strength into the Political Order, but in a Social Order politicized they will not grow. In the earlier stages of the change, if these be conducted with skilled propaganda, there will be an appearance of emotional response, but it is hysteria, induced, not rooted, and certain to wither very quickly. The State cannot confer vitality, for the only vitality it has flows from the spiritual and physical vitality of the human beings of whom it is composed.

13

Caesar and Citizens

We have been telling of Caesar's attitude to Society and the necessity of his understanding what the health of Society requires. But it is important that Society should do a little thinking about Caesar, too—still meaning by Caesar the man or combination of men who wield civil authority. He must not spread into Society's field, but Society must make it possible for him to function in his own. Let us think about him.

(1)

No way has been found, or probably can be found, of getting the best Caesar or even of being sure to get a reasonably good one. No Society has yet tried competitive examination, which is one extreme, or drawing names out of a hat, which is the other (Chesterton has this as England's method of choosing its king in the fifty years hence of *The Napoleon of Notting Hill*). In between those extremes come election, with some vague resemblance to the first, and inheritance, which has elements of the second; these being the commonest but not the only ways of getting your Caesar. With the hereditary ruler you take your chance, with the elected you take your choice.

Experience seems to show that elected rulers are not better than hereditary—not more honourable men, not more competent in government. And there are certain advantages in having your ruler simply provided for you—one of them being that the country has not to be rent asunder every time the highest office falls vacant, another being that which Belloc notes in his *Richelieu,* that hereditary power is the only sort that does not soil the holder in the acquiring of it—where men have to be elected to high office they may be tempted to pull wires unpleasingly and make bargains they despise themselves for making. And, to repeat, election does not balance these disadvantages by producing better Caesars.

But Society, at a certain stage, feels safer with Caesar it appoints and can dismiss, and over whose actions and policies it has therefore more immediate control. The problem it is trying to solve is real—the problem of the Caesar who is a sheer calamity, either because he is tyrannical or because he is incompetent. Upon incompetence, little can be done. You can have a rising of the citizens against him or a *coup d'état* by a small group; but these do not guarantee that the new Caesar will be more competent, since the qualities that make a good leader of a revolt have little bearing on the handling of the enormously complex machinery of life in modern society. You can elect a new Caesar: but the same electors who showed themselves bad judges by choosing the incompetent Caesar will be choosing his successor; and, again, the qualities which make an appealing candidate have as little bearing on the job to be done as those which make a successful revolutionary. But upon tyranny—in the sense of one man imposing his own will against the wishes of the great mass of the citizens—elections *are* something of a safeguard, not perfect but the best that has yet been devised. For they make it possible without bloodshed to be rid of a man whose continuance in office is a threat to Society's freedom. And they make it possible for the citizens as a whole to make their wishes felt in the government of the country. This may or may not be invariably a good thing, but it is inescapable—once a people can read. As soon as they have a general notion of, and their own ideas about, what is going on, in the world at large and in their own world, they must either be consulted or bloodily repressed.

Thus democratic constitutions are aimed at two things: keeping Caesar under control, which is possible, but does not always make for good government, yet is a safeguard against the worst sort of tyranny; and getting the best man for Caesar, which is desirable certainly, but improbable. Let us glance at this a moment. What Society is trying to do is to set up machinery by which it will get a Caesar lacking its own faults—a corrupt Society hopes to get an incorruptible Caesar, a spineless Society a resolute Caesar. But no social machinery will provide virtues that Society lacks: for where should the virtues come from? Not from the machinery, certainly. The real truth is that Caesar *will* represent—that is, be intellectually and morally like, represent as a portrait represents a face—the Society he governs, at any rate in a democracy; even in a monarchy, if it be long established, the chances are that he will be the sort of ruler the average subject would be if the roles were reversed. Even in a revolutionary time there will be a relation: Hitler, for example, was the answer to something in the German people at that moment as a drink is the answer to a thirst. The only way to get a good Caesar is to get a good Society. To get a good Society is a mighty matter, as we have seen and shall see—it means good men, seeing Reality right and striving to live according to their vision.

Meanwhile Societies, our own included, being what they are, Utopianism is foolish. We must settle down to the probability of Caesars no better than ourselves, more or less honest, more or less able. Given the improbability of continuing high ability, it seems sensible not to give Caesar too large a field of operations; certain things *must* be entrusted to him, what need not be probably should not be; his own field is large enough. But, to return to what was said at the opening of this section, within that field we must make it possible for him to function as well as possible.

(2)

Democracy—and it is with democracies of the Western sort that the rest of this book will mainly deal—is not simply a machinery for getting the Caesar you want, and getting rid of him when you find he was not what you wanted after all; it includes as well the idea of some sort of continuing control of Caesar in his governing. A literate citizen body will not be content to elect Caesar, then with a sigh of relief turn back to its own personal affairs leaving public affairs to him. It will have its own ideas about how the life of the state should be conducted, and Caesar must take account of them: against a solid public disapproval, no law can work: against a united public demand, Caesar may be legally entitled to say No but he will not find it easy to say it. The citizens exert a powerful pressure on Caesar: it is essential that they should know their own limitations. When we elect a man to office we do not, if we are sane, elect him to do what we, tyroes, think best but what he, the expert, thinks best. The principle would be obvious in any other field—if I get a doctor, for instance, I do not tell him how my body should be handled, I expect him to tell me. The only reason for not applying the principle to government is the illusion that the body politic requires less expertness than one's own body, that a man must make a special study of the human body and devote his life to its handling and healing, but that anyone and everyone knows all about the body politic without having to study it, and can settle its problems in the odd minutes he can devote to them between his work and his play.

That this is idiotic does not keep it from being almost universal. In his heart, pretty well everyone feels that he could handle affairs of state better than the imbeciles now in charge of them. And if some residual sense of humour prevents his saying actually that, everything he does say breathes the conviction that statesmanship is merely a matter of common sense and good will. During the last war, for instance, one constantly heard that our young men would return from the front determined that this or that evil should no longer afflict society—unemployment, say, or the threat of another world war. It was pathetic to weeping point: as if determination were all that was needed. Determination will never make any machine work, unless one has the necessary skill, born of the necessary study; determination without skill can only smash it. And the State is more complex than any machine, for one reason, because its component parts are human beings—no one of them quite like another, no one of them like himself, even, for long together, and any or all of them capable of working against the whole; for another, because of the complexity of what it has to do—where other machines have one function, one thing to accomplish, the State is concerned with a thing so limitless as the earthly happiness and well-being of the incalculable beings who compose it.

A myriad factors enter, and all must be understood—the balance between agriculture and heavy industry, for instance, with the effect of each upon physical and spiritual health, the danger to a country that concentrates all upon heavy industry so that it must import its food and may be starved in war time, and the danger to a country so set upon the agricultural life that it has not enough heavy industries to provide the munitions, so that it cannot defend itself; or the balance between various sections of the community, so that no one of them is able to use the State for the exploitation of the others; the problems of Capital and Management and Labour; the appallingly difficult, perhaps insoluble, problem of money and credit. Nothing that the medical doctor has to handle is more obscure than the problems of the Statesman. Even if there were no such thing as Foreign Affairs, the conduct of the State would require a high degree of intelligence and knowledge and technical skill, not to be acquired in odd hours as a hobby, but a lifework.

And, as it happens, there *are* Foreign Affairs. And they are very difficult. Few things are more depressing than to hear a group of citizens solving the larger political problems of mankind with no qualifications other than the couple of drinks they have just absorbed. The immediate problems are bad enough—whether a boundary-line should be drawn at some river the citizen has never heard of, whether a racial minority whose existence he had not so much as suspected should go in with one great power or another, what the consequences will be of this or that course of action—how Nation A will react, whether Nation B will feel compelled to exert pressure upon Nation C, just what do Nations A and B and C regard as vital interests and why. As I say, the immediate problems are bad enough, but they are not to be approached at all without a knowledge of history, the whole of the past is an element in every present situation.

Every nation acts by all sorts of motives and impulses connected with its past, a sort of national memory, and unless you know what is in the national memory, it will seem to be acting on no motive at all, but quite irrationally. America knows what Plymouth Rock and George Washington and Abraham Lincoln are in the American memory, and one who has never heard of them will find America to that extent incomprehensible. To the outsider Irish policy often seems sheerly, even maddeningly, perverse: simply because in Ireland's national memory are Queen Elizabeth and Oliver Cromwell: at every conference between Irish and English those two are present, and operative: the English do not know it and therefore are never quite clear what is happening.

Every country has its national memory, conditioning its here-and-now decisions. But not only what it remembers, all that has happened to it is a factor. For the statesman, the capital question is, What is Russia going to do? Even Stalin does not know. How is a tree going to grow? The gardener knows what he wants and so does Stalin. But the gardener knows he may get something very different. So, I suppose, does Stalin. There is the same principle in both instances. You cannot do what you like with anything: you can only do what can be done with it. And with a living thing what can be done with it depends on what life has already done to it. You can to some extent shape its future: but not if you ignore its past. Try to shape the future of a man, and all that has ever happened to him will be working with you or against you—mostly against you, unless you are very wise. So with a people. So with the Russian people.

We of the outer world are not trying to shape Russia but only to foresee what she will do. We must study Communism, which is the new element in the situation; but it is still more important to know the history of Russia. And most of us do not. We may fear Russia as a threat or hail Russia as a promise; the chances are that we could not pass the simplest examination in Russian history. Think how funny that is. English nurses used to scare babies with the bogey-man Napoleon. Nurses still thrill babies with the promise of Santa Claus. We are horribly like babies with our pathetic fears or hopes, knowing precious little more about Russia than the babies know about Napoleon or Santa Claus, but listening hollow-eyed or shining-eyed to the dear old nurses who write the editorials and are as ignorant as we. For if you do not know a country's history, you do not know the country. If you do not know what kind of things it has done and what have been its dominant motives over the long span of its history, how can you have the faintest notion of what kind of things it is going to do and upon what motives? Emotional reactions to what one has heard of its last twenty years are not enough.

I have been jotting down at random some of the elements that go to make up Caesar's job, in ruling his own country and handling its relations with others. The great mass of the citizens know nothing of them. A small minority know a little: they make a serious effort to keep abreast, but too many things keep taking place, one drives another out of the front of the mind, where things are clearly known, into the back of the mind, where the thing called General Knowledge lives its half-life—a chaos of the things we once knew, their skeletons picked by time and piled in some strange order that is not the order of their being or happening. No doctor whose memory of his medical studies was one-tenth so confused would dare to prescribe for a sore finger.

And this is the serious minority. The great mass of us know nothing of such things now and never have known anything. A recent Gallup Poll enquiry put six questions to a cross section of the adult population of the United States. (1) Where is Manchuria? (2) Where is Formosa? (3) What is meant by the 38th Parallel? (4) What is meant by the Atlantic Pact? (5) Who is Chiang Kai-shek? (6) Who is Marshal Tito? The questions are so elementary, and the answers have so filled the newspapers for the past year, that even a man who answered them all would have proved nothing as to his competence for judgment upon foreign affairs; but only 12% could answer them all; and 19% could not answer any. The Report goes on to say that in June 1951, when the Iranian oil question was front page news throughout the world, only 40% of Americans knew where Iran was. And a similar enquiry upon America's domestic policies produced a result no more cheerful.

The general ignorance of domestic and foreign problems may be no greater today than in the past, but it is complicated for us by one new factor. Everyone reads digests, sees films, listens to radio commentators: so that people have the illusion that they know everything, whereas they have only heard of everything. Not only that. They have views about things on which they lack the elements of knowledge—not their own views, but acquired from some convincing writer or speaker. They have lent their ears, perhaps, to a politician of the camp opposed to Caesar, who may be honest and competent but who certainly wants to get Caesar out and himself in. Or to a publicist—a writer of books or radio commentator—and he is probably honest, he is not likely to be competent (since the nature of his work allows neither for the study of the fundamentals nor for the practical handling of public affairs which combine to produce competence), and in any event he is driven by the necessity, imperious beyond all others, of being interesting: for that is his living. Or to one of those men with a theory that solves everything—Social Credit, for instance, or a world-wide Jewish conspiracy, or the Materialist Interpretation of History, or Bi-metalism, or Back to the Land—his theory may be sound, though universal solutions seldom are and their propounders too often have the secret smile of the slightly mad. All of these people, hundreds of them, thousands of them, are shouting at Caesar. And it is all insane. A given politician, publicist, universal solutionist, may have the truth: they cannot all have it, for they contradict one another: still, one or other of them may have it. But 95% of the citizens are quite incompetent to judge whether it is the truth or not. Which does not stop them bringing pressure on Caesar.

What is Caesar supposed to do? For the most part, one imagines, he is philosophical about it: issues come and go, today's paper lights tomorrow's fire: and public opinion is a great roar, with a myriad tongues contributing, and no utterance. But every so often some one shout rises above the rest and soon all seem to be shouting it. And then is the fateful moment for Caesar. The public demands a course of action which Caesar knows will be disastrous. In theory, there is no problem. He was elected to govern the country, not to be governed by it. He must do what he sees as best for the country. If a man asks me for arsenic, I waste no time on theoretic discussion of his right to poison himself, I will not give it to him. If he will not be denied, he must get his arsensic from someone else. A ruler is not a pander. Public opinion is not recognized by any constitution as a partner in the actual conduct of the country's affairs (though certain matters, usually involving changes in the constitutional structure, may be reserved to the public by way of plebiscite). Caesar must do what he thinks best. If in the end he finds that public opinion is too strong for him, and he cannot carry his own policies against it, he may decide to resign and let someone else provide the arsenic: though here he must weigh the question who will take his place, and may decide that, if arsenic the public must have, it had better after all have it administered by a man who knows that arsenic is poison.

(3)

But I come back to the point. Since public opinion has this power, it is shameful that the public should do so little to equip themselves for its exercise. Probably if they equipped themselves better, they would be tempted to exercise it less. For there is a paradox at the root of it. The ground of our interference is that Caesar is either evil or incompetent: but *we* chose him. To interfere with Caesar in *his* job is, as we have already noted, to admit that we have already been incompentent in our own.

To choose honest, competent men should not be beyond our powers. If we are incapable of that, how are we likely to be capable of handling problems that stretch so far beyond our knowledge and experience? To that primarily the electors must devote themselves. We should soberly study the candidates as men, really weighing their actions and words, not being fooled by glibness of tongue in a politician any more than we should in a business-man, not choosing a man we should not trust in private life. We should study parties and their principles, which includes studying their past performances both in themselves and in relation to the principles professed. We should watch the way the life of the country is going, for though we cannot all be experts in politics, any more than in medicine, we should be able to judge whether the body politic, or our own body, is healthy and growing healthier or diseased and growing worse. We cannot be judges of the processes, but we can know if the product is what we want.

Now it would be idle to pretend that most citizens go about the choosing of Caesar in that way. There is an immense amount of habit, self-interest, old prejudice, excitability, suggestibility. Above all there is so much preoccupation with one's job and one's amusements that there are only odd half-hours left for studying parties and candidates. The duty to vote is a duty to equip oneself to vote. For the man who has not taken the trouble, there is a duty not to vote. Democracy is no magic formula by which wise decisions are extracted from blank ignorance.

Is the function of the citizens in a democracy solely to elect? That is their clearest function, and the one which distinguishes democracies from other polities. But it is not their first function. The duty they must at all costs perform is to create the moral and spiritual atmosphere in which Caesar must operate—if they do not, their care in electing will go for nought; if they do, even bad Caesars will be not so bad. Public opinion as to the best way of handling a foreign problem, or as to the best way of financing some great scheme within the country, has no more value than the amount of relevant knowledge the public has. But where public opinion can be valid is in setting up standards of right and wrong, of tolerable and intolerable, and holding to them so firmly that Caesar has no choice but to act by them. If public opinion upon corruption is so clear that the politician proved corrupt vanishes from political life, then corruption will become exceptional. If the public would be horrified and humiliated by the betrayal of an ally, then allies will not so often be betrayed. If the public reacts against cruelty instantly and vigorously, then subject populations will not be butchered and the destitute at home will not be left to starve.

At present in most democracies, public opinion is a mixture, sensitive to some evils, insensitive to others. Observing a given nation's policy in one matter, one feels it has no conscience at all, and no guide but expediency: yet in a different matter it will act most morally. The reason is as I have said: the public opinion of that country is not alive on the one matter and very much alive on the other. Caesar is a practical man and a busy man: he will tend to solve problems in their own terms, without reference to considerations of general morality. If the public does not keep the standards clear, there will be no standards. To be working for a public opinion, in this sense healthy and responsive, is the duty of every citizen.

It may be the duty of some citizens to devote themselves especially to it—to clarifying the principles by which men live and to uttering them so that all may hear and be won to them. Choosing politicians is not the only way in which a man can do his duty as a citizen: working for a healthy public opinion is more important still. No man can do everything; and if a given man devotes himself so wholly to the establishing of the right standards that he has no time for the study of the men and the issues at election time, Society is not the loser. Society indeed may be the gainer by good men who go out from it altogether, as the Hermits did: since, from the prayer which is their whole life, the welfare of society is not excluded. When St. Paul the Hermit, after close on a century of total solitude, was visited by St. Anthony, his first question was

"Tell me, I pray you, how fares the human race: if new roofs be risen in the ancient cities; whose empire is it that now sways the world?" How fared the human race? Ill enough, doubtless, but the better for that century of solitary prayer. There are many ways of serving the community of our fellows. Only the man who has no care at all for Society, to whom it is solely a convenience, a means to his end, is cheating—not repaying in service all the manifold service that Society renders him, cutting himself off wholly from the love which, in the social order as in every order, is the secret of life.

14

Liberty, Equality, Personality

The standards that Society should establish are not only moral standards, though these are the most important, but the scale of values generally—what things are valued, and in what order. To take a rough example: there is a river, clear, clean, beautiful; on its banks a man proposes to build a factory for the making of shoe-polish, whereby the water will be polluted and the beauty of the scenery ruined. There are three values involved: beautiful scenery is a value: polished shoes are a value: money is a value. In the nineteenth century our own society invariably let the man build the factory: not, I imagine, because they thought polished shoes a higher value than beautiful scenery, but because they thought money a higher value than beauty. Wrong values of this sort are always serious, but a healthy society, like a healthy man, can take a surprising number of liberties with the laws of health and not die of them. Provided Caesar and society have the same scale of values, things can rub along well enough in spite of very curious misvaluations.

But there is one value on which they must be right, or all is in peril: it is sociologically the primary value, the standard of standards, the human person. It is the *raison d'être* of Society and State. They exist because without them man cannot be all that is in him to be, cannot indeed be fully man, but undeveloped or mis-developed, truncated or distorted. The one test of their worth is the degree in which they serve man. And they can only serve man if they are right about what he is. Is man, by their operation, more of a man or less of a man?

Neither governors nor governed will keep the service of man as their primary purpose, unless they see *man as primary*.

They will not know how to serve him, unless they see *man as he is*.

A right vision of man shows both why he should be served and how he is to be served; for it shows him as an object of reverence, and it shows what things will help and what hinder a being of that sort in becoming what he is meant to be and achieving what he is meant to achieve.

The sort of being man is was discussed at length in the first section. I shall summarize some of the things said there, and expand others. Man is a being created by God, living in a universe created by God, living therefore wholly under God's laws. He is linked by powers and needs to his fellow-men. In himself he is a union of spirit and matter: by his spirit, immortal and made in God's image; his body too God's handiwork; both matter and spirit essential to the fulness of his personality. By his spirit, man knows and loves, is free to choose, and by the choices he makes is responsible for his own eternal well- or ill-being. By his very essence, then, he is free and responsible. He can misuse his freedom and responsibility, and may have to be checked; but his development is bound up with learning to use them aright. He grows in manhood by growing in freedom and responsibility; he is diminished in manhood by their diminution. He can have his freedom diminished either by his own misuse of it or by the interference of others; his own misuse damages his powers of choice and action in themselves, wrongful interference damages them by diminishing the area in which he should be allowed to exercise them.

One way or another, the rest of this book will be concerned with the question how man, thus seen, fits into the order of Society and State. The very word "order" tells us that there must be interference, you will not get order among human beings without giving orders: when is interference wrongful? Authority commands and forbids: how shall it serve freedom?

(1)

Any action by the State, we have seen, that hinders the development of man, that makes a man less of a man, is simply monstrous. And this is so, even if it is done with the best intentions. There have been bad Caesars and mad Caesars like Heliogabalus and Hitler, the world has never lacked them and does not lack them now: that they are monstrous needs no showing here. But in the Western democracies—whom I have principally in mind throughout this section, Britain and America particularly—the main threat is not from such as these. It is from rulers honourably intent upon the Common Good, but misconceiving it.

And indeed it is easy to misconceive. *So many things would obviously be for the Common Good, which yet it would be against the Common Good to command by law.*

It would, for example, be a wonderful thing for Society if all marriages were happy, but a ghastly business if Caesar undertook to make them so. If the State decided who should marry whom, upon reports from anatomists and bio-chemists and psychiatrists and statisticians, it would be denying a human right compared with which its own is secondary indeed, and treating its members not like men but like animals in a stud farm.

It would, for another example, be for the Common Good if all men were models of physical fitness, but if Caesar tried to make them so—by compulsory daily exercises, a compulsory diet, and statutory hours in bed—he would be acting against the Common Good, to which it is essential that the citizens should be responsible men, not babies in dribble-bibs, nursemaided by Caesar.

Let us take a third example, cutting deeper than either of the others. It has been our thesis throughout that Society cannot be really united, if it is not united on the fundamental question of what man is, which involves the further question of the meaning and goal of life, and the standard by which we shall know what actions are right and what wrong. In other words, it would obviously be for the Common Good if all citizens had the same religion—but only if they had accepted it for themselves, not if the State had forced them to. We can see this at two levels.

At the first level, it is obvious that Caesar must not force them. It is not his job to impose the values he holds on Society. Thus if a Mohammedan ruler tries to force Mohammedanism upon his Christian subjects, we tell him that he is acting wrongly, not because Islam is a false religion, but because it is not his business as Caesar to impose a religion. Similarly if a Christian ruler tried to force Christianity upon Mohammedan subjects, the fact that Christianity is the true religion does not make it Caesar's business to impose it. And what I have said of force, would apply to any other undue exercise of State power—as by making it worth men's while socially, economically or politically as Julian the Apostate did and scores of rulers since, to embrace Caesar's religion.

But if it might be agreed without much difficulty that *Caesar* cannot impose his religious views upon the Society he rules, is it as clear whether *Society* has a right to impose its religious views upon its individual members? Where a given religion is held at once pretty universally and very ardently, then the whole force of public opinion may make life difficult for a minority that does not agree, and there is not much that can be done about this—immediately anyhow. The deep-lying attitudes of a people are beyond anybody's control, and so are the social pressures that public opinion almost automatically exercises. But what I am raising is a different question—whether Society is *entitled* to enforce its dominant religious outlook upon everybody? It is clear that religion, which is man's relation to God, belongs to the area of choice and can only grow stunted and mechanical under compulsion. It could never be anything but grave profanation to enforce a religion upon any man—as, for example, Christianity was forced upon pagan Saxons by Charlemagne, and Mohammedanism upon Christian Moors by Idris. That the Saxons ultimately settled down well enough as Christians no more excuses the profanation than that the Moors ultimately settled down well enough as Mohammedans.

Quite apart from an individual's own right in the matter, the nature of religion is contradicted by compulsion.

It would be simpler if one could rule out marriage and health and religion, and all other such primarily personal questions, as out of bounds for the State (especially the neutral State with which we are mainly concerned). But that would be to oversimplify. A man's relations with women, his handling of his body, his attitude to God, are essentially his own affair: yet what he does about them cannot stay within the close confines of his own personality, but must have far-reaching effects upon others. The rights of those others are implicated in them, the Common Good is implicated in them, the State has a right to legislate for them, it would be failing in its duty if it left health or marriage or religion unregarded. Thus a man has a right to choose his own wife and, if she be willing, marry her and have children by her; but if he wants to have two wives at once, then the State will intervene, if it sees monogamy as of Society's very structure. A man may handle his own body with every sort of unwisdom to his undoing; but he must not infect others: the State is not acting tyrannously if it insists upon vaccination or makes him install a reasonable drainage system. What a man believes about God is a matter upon which he cannot be coerced, but his religion may involve external conduct which the State cannot ignore—from simple matters like refusing on conscientious grounds to pay taxes or wear clothes, to horrors like suttee, the Hindu custom by which when a man died his wives were burned alive.

Where, then, must the line be drawn between laws the State is entitled to make and laws that would be, to use our earlier word, monstrous? The growing modern tendency is to apply the single rule that the Common Good must take precedence over the interests and even the rights of the individual. But that is an oversimplification in the other direction: for the Common Good *cannot* be served by diminishing men as men: the individual may be called on to make sacrifices, but not of his manhood.

What we seek is a principle, one that is rooted securely in the nature of man, to settle for us where the State is entitled to intervene and where the individual must be left to make his own decisions. For the Christian, it should be easy. But it is not. Certain things stand out very clearly, but not all things. Let us see how far we can walk with certainty. The State cannot rightly make any law that contradicts the Law of God; we have already seen and shall see again how tremendous a defence of human freedom is here. Nor can it rightly make any law that denies the rights of man: as we have seen, these *are* rights, not concessions: a man may so misuse his rights as to forfeit them, so invade the rights of others as to lose the right to invoke the protection of his own; but if we can alienate our own rights, no one can take them from us. The Common Good cannot possibly be served by ignoring either of these principles, for in the first place they are part of the order of reality, and to deny reality is folly: and in any event the Common Good must go limpingly without them, for the order of morality is essential to it, and the sacredness of the rights of each man is the indispensable condition of the well-being of all.

Can we go one step further and say that, provided the Law of God and the fundamental rights of man are not infringed, the State may exercise any control it pleases upon the individual, for the good of all? To cast back to the examples we have already used, the State is not invading human rights when it forbids bigamy or suttee, demands that citizens pay their taxes, protect themselves against smallpox, wear clothes. To say yes is tempting. Such a principle would be a great deal better than no principle at all, which is what most countries have at present. But it is not enough, all the same.

For, if a principle is what we are seeking, this will not do! It looks like a principle, but it is not; for it is based upon an assumption—namely, that if a man cannot establish a right to do this or that, the State has a right to stop him. But this cannot be assumed. The absence of a right in one party does not establish the presence of a right in the other. If a man, asserting a right, may be called upon to prove he has it, so may the State. It is a question, as the lawyers say, where the residuary right lies, or perhaps where the onus of proof lies. Has the State got (I don't mean constitutionally but morally) all rights which the individual cannot prove to be his? Or has the individual got all the rights which the State cannot prove to be its? There is no question which way the current is running. Shall we be satisfied to let it run? In other words, even if our principle is not a principle, will it do as a working rule?

The answer must again be no. For, first, it is not always easy, when we come down to details, to establish what the rights of man are in a given matter—not easy for ourselves, to say nothing of the many-religioned and no-religioned Society to which we belong; and, second, such a rule would not necessarily save the one thing that must be saved, man's freedom and responsibility—it would be quite possible to weaken our powers of decision and initiative by controls and interferences without infringing any of our clearly provable fundamental rights.

Concentrate for a moment upon the first of these reasons —the difficulty of establishing in every case what the rights of man are. Examples must serve here, instead of the whole book a proper discussion would require.

Apart from the protection of monogamy, which belongs to the social structure, how far is the State entitled to legislate on sexual conduct? You cannot make men moral by Act of Parliament; and even if you could, you would not be entitled to; morality lies in the free choice of the will, whatever is not freely chosen is not morality. But if the law cannot stop sin where it belongs, in the inaccessible depths of the human will, it can—that is, it is physically able to—forbid the external actions in which the sinful will expresses itself. How far should it do so? Our own State, like most others, does not forbid pre-marital intercourse, but leaves it to the responsibility of the individual conscience. On the other hand, it does forbid homosexuality. Yet both are sins against the law of God. Similarly, in most of the Western world, polygamy is forbidden, but not prostitution: yet, again, both are sins against the law of God.

In all this, is Society acting on any principle at all? Not one principle, certainly, but two, in incalculable combination. The first is that while no one has a right to sin, it does not follow that anyone (God always excepted) has any right to stop another sinning: and, even if he has, it may not be a good thing to exercise the right, because the interference thus made necessary might give rise to further evils. Thus St. Augustine argues that prostitution should not be suppressed because worse evils might follow, and Leo XIII (in *Libertas praestantissimum*) generalizes the principle, "Public authority may tolerate [not, of course, do] what is at variance with truth and justice, to avoid some greater evil or to obtain and preserve some greater good." In any event, compulsion is not usually best for the sinner's character. For the most part, the State does not normally stop sinners damaging themselves by sin—as in pre-marital intercourse: it stops them only when their sin involves a direct aggression upon others.

What then of the almost universal prohibition of homosexual intercourse? Here we come to the other principle, whose combination with the first I have called incalculable. It is this, that a Society will always react violently in defence of what it holds to be vital interests. Where things are done which the generality of men see either as repulsive in themselves, or as a threat to the well-being or fundamental structure of Society, fine distinctions will not be drawn about the rights of man and the personal responsibility of the individual. Society will always protect itself and if necessary call upon the State by force to protect it, against whatever threatens either its existence or, what comes very near the same thing, its fundamental structure and the values by which it lives. It will call upon the State to use force to resist an aggressor from without or a sedition from within, because both these things threaten its existence. Similarly it will call upon the State to act against those who, for example, deny the right of civil authority or any institution which it conceives as basic, such as marriage, or property, or free speech; or against those who violently contradict the *mores*—by homosexuality, for instance, or incest, or any other action it feels to be beyond the pale and abominable. And it will call upon the State to take action against such assaults on its fundamental principles, whether the assault is conducted in the name of religion or in some other name: in this matter, the question of religion is merely incidental. What Society is resisting is a threat to what it conceives as its own intimate and ultimate well-being. Thus the United States Congress forbade the polygamy which the Mormon revelation declared to be a command of God: the Mormons may understandably have seen this as religious persecution, but Congress did not mean it so. It was the same with the British prohibition of suttee in India, the principle of the prohibition being that the burning of innocent women is in itself abominable, no matter what the reason advanced. I think it will be found that most of the so-called religious persecutions of history have been of this sort—Society not so much trying to impose its own religion or destroy another, as to meet what it saw as a mortal threat—its religion being so intertwined with its life that in defending its religion it felt it was fighting for its life. This, one hastens to add, would have been no consolation to the martyrs at the time and does not dim the glory of their heroism now.

Because the threat is seen as mortal, Society's reaction strikes the detached onlooker, not himself mortally threatened, as exaggerated, even hysterical. But we should not too hastily condemn. The instinct of self-preservation has to be strong, even violent, or the organism, individual or social, will perish. The healthiest organisms react most vigorously. Under the microscope nothing could look more hysterical than a rush of phagocytes to combat bacteria in the blood stream! Do not deprecate their vehemence, your survival depends upon it. When an organism reacts for its own preservation, the trouble is not in the vehemence but in the possibility of error, to which phagocytes are not liable, but men are. A society may misconceive its own vital interests, and see itself threatened where there is no threat—as the Roman Empire tried for three centuries to destroy Christianity, which was in the end its salvation. The *mores* it is defending may be any sort of hodge-podge of sound, unsound and plainly grotesque, inherited from a long past and by now inveterate, so that the average citizen is all but incapable of calling them in question. And in the energy of its reaction it may trample human rights underfoot, sinning against the reverence due to man.

What is to be the attitude of the assailed minority? They have no grievance against Society for differing from them about its own vital interests, or God's will, or man's nature. It sometimes happens, though not invariably as the sentimentalist thinks, that Society is in the wrong of it and the minority in the right: even then, it is no reasonable accusation against any people that it is not infallible. The wronged few may decide to bear with the evil, using every opportunity to bring their fellows to a truer view. Or the challenge may be so presented that they must face it and accept imprisonment, exile or death. The spirit in which they do so is of an importance that cannot be exaggerated. The martyr, of course, sees that he himself can do no other. It is better still if he sees that Society can do no other, either—the tenth-century Mohammedan mystic al-Hallaj, about to be crucified by the leaders of his own religion, prayed for them, "these Thy servants who are gathered to slay me, in zeal for Thy religion and in desire to win Thy favour." It is best of all if his love for the people that has cast him out is not diminished but increased: then indeed he is dying not only for his cause but for his people, and his death works for the renewal of Society. Surprisingly often love *is* increased. It was so with al-Hallaj, it has been so with Christian martyrs through the ages: all but heartbreaking are the protestations of love for England and the Queen uttered by the martyrs who died under Elizabeth Tudor. Christ Our Lord set them the example, "Jerusalem, Jerusalem, thou that killest the prophets and stonest them that are sent unto thee, how often would I have gathered together thy children, as the mother bird gathers her young under her wings, and thou wouldst not."

What seems clear is that we cannot draw up two lists, one of matters the State may handle, one of matters inviolably individual. Certain things we see are clearly within the State's competence; certain things as clearly outside it. Between lies a vast border region where we cannot be guided by set rules, but only by healthy instincts arising from a true vision of reality. Provided the instincts are healthy and the vision true it does not matter greatly whether Caesar takes a little more or a little less. Perfect balance is not for us, imperfect men with rulers imperfect too. The essential thing, once more, is that governors and governed should keep the meaning of man steadily in mind. Left to himself, man has always, rightly, reserved the noun and the adjective manly to the man with certain special qualities—the resolute man, capable of decision, tenacious in execution, not frightened of responsibility: in the degree in which he lacks these qualities, man is less of a man; if he be incapable of decision and therefore of responsibility, he seems hardly a man at all. That society justifies itself which values those essential things in man and cherishes them in its members: in *all* its members.

(2)

Which brings us to the other great test question, the question of equality. In the first section we looked at the truth that all men are equal to see what it meant; we must look at it again to see what its effects are upon life in Society.

All men are equal in the same way as all triangles are equal. One triangle (to repeat our earlier illustration) may be made of platinum and one of putty, so that there is accidental inequality; but in all that goes with being triangles there is equality: they each have three sides, in each any two sides are greater than the third side, the angles of each total 180°. In man it is the same: there is accidental inequality—of strength, intelligence, energy, skill. But in all that goes with being a man there is equality —each man is an immortal spirit, each is in God's image, Christ died for all. The only question is whether the element in which there is equality is more important or less important than the element in which there is inequality. One might very well say that all this talk of the equality of the two triangles is true but pointless: the difference between platinum and putty far outweighs the elements of similarity. I personally would choose the platinum every time, leaving the other for the geometricians to revel in. But if one does the same with the man, the consequences are bound to be catastrophic. Almost instinctively we do do the same, and the consequences are catastrophic. We judge men by their differences and write off the equality as of no consequence. If ever Christ's plea is valid that men be forgiven because they knew not what they do, it is valid here. We simply could not do it, if we knew what we were doing. The difference between platinum and putty matters more than that between triangle and circle: but no natural difference between one man and another compares for an instant with the splendour of that which all men have. If we find this or that difference between men more impressive than spirit and immortality and the love of God and the blood of Christ, we are so divorced from the reality of things that we cannot possibly act sanely.

The first fact that should strike us about anyone and everyone is that he is a human person, a man. And provided that we have a healthy rightness about what a man is, that is already tremendous. It means that we see him as a person—one who is, under God, an end in himself—and not a thing—to be used for the convenience of others; it means that we see him as an object of reverence, having in his nature the original sacredness that goes with likeness to God, and the access of sacredness that comes from redemption by Christ.

If we can look at any man and not see that, it means that we undervalue manhood; we either do not know at all what is involved in being a man, or we do not know it as a living truth. Just as by allowing divorce we weaken the whole idea of marriage, including our own; so by slavery or any use of man as simply a means to our end, by snobbery or any value attached to accidental superiorities to the eclipse of fundamental equality, we degrade the whole idea of manhood, including our own. *"Nihil humani a me alienum puto,"* said Terence with a beautiful precision—Whatever touches any man concerns *me:* and St. Paul "Who is weak, and I am not weak?" lifts this reality in the natural order to a higher level. If man as such does not matter, then I as man do not matter—I bank everything on the accidentals in which I fancy myself superior to other men. God help me.

But if the accidental differences matter less than the substantial equality, they are a fact all the same; they are part of reality, and no part of reality can be ignored. There are differences between men and women, for instance, and between poets and scientists; and if such differences as these raise no problem of superior and inferior, there are plenty that do—differences in energy, or intelligence, or knowledge, or skill, or civic virtue. In the life of Society the equality of men is fundamental; but the differences must be realistically and therefore fruitfully used. That a man is made in the image of God does not of itself mean that he can teach, or construct bridges, or control the country's finances. It does not even mean that he can vote intelligently. All these things and a thousand others are *functions,* which must be performed adequately or Society will suffer; and no one can perform them merely in virtue of being a man. It is no insult to human equality to say that certain men or groups within the body politic are not equipped for the fulness of citizenship. It is simply a question of fact—are they or are they not equipped?

But if the answer is no, we cannot stop there. Two questions arise. Does their insufficiency affect their wholeness as men? And is it Society's fault, and by Society's act remediable? If a group have been so maltreated by Society that they have been denied the possibility of full development as men, then we cannot rest content with establishing the fact: we should be striving for the remedy. It should be impossible to look unmoved upon men, made in God's image and loved by Christ to the sacrifice of His own life, but deformed and dehumanized by man's action or neglect. And this is not only true of groups. Any single human being is a challenge to us to co-operate in the development of whatever powers are in him. To wrap our own talents in a napkin is a sin for which God will judge us; so to wrap the talents of others is hardly likely to please God more.

But however determined we may be that a certain sort of damage in ourselves and others shall be healed, pending healing it remains a fact, and there is no gain in ignoring facts. And, with however much healing, there will remain inequalities in social function and inequalities in reward. In this sense there can be no such thing as equality, and the effort to secure equality is in its essence folly and in its results can do great harm.

I call it folly. There can be no such thing as equality in power. By law you can give each man one vote. But a man who has the skill to make the speeches or the slogans that influence a million voters really casts a million votes, and there is no way of stopping him, short of a total stifling of every voice save Caesar's.

So obvious is this that the champions of equality are forced to concentrate their equalizing efforts upon the reward: no man shall receive more recompense than another. But they have left men out of account. How can you measure the reward that a poet or a scientist gets *from* his work, as distinct from what he is paid for doing it? There is a joy and an agony in the exercise of his powers, a development of himself in their exercise, an alternation of joy in his accomplishment because it is good and anguish because it might have been better. You could drive yourself mad trying to devise an accounting system that would cover all that: the one thing certain is that money has precious little bearing on it: he would still be striving and agonizing and rejoicing, if he were never to receive a penny for it: and millions in royalties would not compensate him for his own ultimate certainty that he had failed.

Indeed for so many of the things people devote their lives to doing, money is either no part, or no decisive part, of the reward. There is the factor we have already mentioned, satisfaction in the work done, and no way of ensuring to all equal shares of that. There is the esteem of one's fellows—the man who influences public opinion is honoured and rejoices in the honour; the writer and the sculptor and the painter and the architect and the lecturer hope that their work will be admired, and rejoice when it is; the wife cooks with a good heart if her husband appreciates her cooking. The esteem and admiration of others loom large in man's life, and so they should: not largest of all, but large: it would be vanity, of course, to make them a motive for action, to act simply in order to win them, but it would be pride to despise them. God Himself wants men's love and men's honour, and it can hardly be beneath *our* dignity to be pleased by them.

But there is no way of ensuring that all men shall be esteemed and admired and loved equally. So that the equality-at-all-costs people must narrow their equalizing efforts still further, and concentrate them upon one single element—the material rewards for labour, money, in short, or money's worth. To re-distribute material goods because the excessive wealth of some gives them too much power in the State may be reasonable. If their excess means that some lack sufficiency, to re-distribute is not only reasonable but obligatory: for many to starve that some may surfeit is intolerable. But to do it out of a mere passion for equality, means that we are back at the vulgarity of a material measuring-rod for success: with spiritual goods not regarded as goods at all. Money is worthless as a measuring-rod for success. For a man to be a success, not in this or that particular field but in life as a whole—to be a successful *man,* and not simply a successful trader or fighter or burglar or doctor or politician—means two things, a primary and a consequent. The primary is that he has built himself into a man, the completest man he had it in him to become—he is not just a bundle of human ingredients loosely slung together, but a fully formed human being, integrated in himself and with his fellows, all his powers functioning at their maximum. In the assessment of that, money does not figure at all. It figures no more in the other meaning of success, the consequent, that man has found satisfaction. This is an easier test to apply than the other, whether to oneself or someone else; for dissatisfaction is not easy to conceal, and a dissatisfied man is obviously not a success, whatever the list of his achievements.

I have called this a consequent, and so it is. Satisfaction—better called joy—is bound up essentially with what one is and only sketchily with what one has. One man can get more joy out of a few pennies spent on a Shakespeare play or a Mozart record than another out of a yacht that has cost him a million. A young man can get more joy out of his bride than the Chinese war lord, with all the women in the region at his disposal, desperately trying to regain his lost virility by drinking tiger's blood. Joy is always a question of one's own power to respond. The universe is all about us, offering delight in a myriad ways if we can respond. Development as a man brings with it the development of our responses—responses to light and line and colour, to physical beauty and spiritual, to music and poetry and sculpture, to the hundred excellences of other men and women, to truth as it embodies the mystery of Reality challenging the mind to solve it or calling the mind to contemplate it. No one responds to everything the universe has to offer, but joy lies in the responses we have, and is measured by their value and variety and intensity: education is the process of developing our responses. In so rich a universe, the man who cannot be happy without a luxury yacht is like a tone-deaf man doing a crossword puzzle at a symphony concert.

One can see why men who have known the bite of destitution should feel, fiercely, that equality of ownership is the one solution. But given the different capacities and the different desires of men, it cannot be achieved without a constant prying and vast interference by the State with the life of the individual. In the end it can only mean that the State owns everything, and the citizens use things as it allows them. And that is too great a price to pay. The tyranny of the nineteenth century was by the rich; but the main threat of tyranny in the twentieth is from the State. To be solely concerned with fighting the battle of the nineteenth century is a sure way to lose the battle of the twentieth.

The price, one sees, is too great—even if equality of material goods were worth achieving. But is it? Provided I have enough, what does it matter if some other men have too much? If I am troubled about it, the reason will almost certainly be envy—I'm as good as he is, why should he? . . . why shouldn't I? . . . It is a feeling common enough in small children: but the adult should be on his guard against it, for it is mere meanness. We can feel sorry for the man harried by envy, but we will not turn the life of Society upside down to soothe him.

Provided every man has enough—that is the key to it. *Enough*—whatever is required for life and adequacy of life: *every* man—no man excluded from the reverence due to the human person, no man denied the rights of man. In a given society the rights of man can have no more value than man himself. If he is seen as different from the lower animals not in kind but only in degree of development, it is derisory to speak of fundamental rights at all. Fundamental rights are meaningless in a being of no fundamental significance. This is what really matters, to establish the worth of the human person. It is small gain to assert that all men are equal, if all are equal to nothing much.

(3)

As we have seen, there is an organic meaning for the phrase "rights of man." It does not mean

What men would like to have,
or what men can manage to get,
or what the State thinks it can safely allow them.

It means what man must have in order to function fully and freely as men. We can list the rights of man,* and

* Pius XI, for example, does so in *Divini Redemptoris:* "The right to

it is good that we should, good too that we should draw up a code—formalized as a constitution or generalized as a way of life—by which the Common Good is served and the rights of man safeguarded.

But, as the first two sections of this chapter have tried to show, list and code will not work automatically, so to speak. Far more important than studying the programme or memorizing the list is grasping the principles that give validity to both, namely the law of God and the nature of man, especially of man as a person, free and responsible. When things go tranquilly, the code suffices, though even then, since nothing in this imperfect world is perfect, it cannot cover all possible cases, and in any event a developing view of man may show defects in it. But in changing times, it is not enough to stand firm upon the code. In so far as it is meant to express that arrangement of the things of this world most harmonious with the nature of man, and therefore best directed to serve both the individual citizen and the common good, it may need restatement as circumstances change. Thus, for example, the Catholic Church holds that men have a right to possess and use private property. But in the encyclical *Quadragesimo Anno,* Pope Pius XI noted that, as things now are, "certain forms of property must be reserved for the State, since they carry with them a power too great to be left to private individuals without injury to the community at large. When civil authority adjusts ownership to meet the needs

---

life, to bodily integrity, to obtain the necessary means of existence; the right to tend towards his ultimate goal in the path marked out for him by God; the right of association and the right to possess and use property. Just as matrimony and the right to its natural use are of Divine origin, so likewise are the constitution and fundamental prerogatives of the family fixed and determined by the Creator."

of the public good, it acts not as the enemy but as the friend of private owners."

In normal times, with social and economic realities changing at a reasonable pace nothing more is involved than adjustment of the rights listed in the code. But in times of crisis, war for instance or famine, Society may not be able to live by the code at all, but only by the principles. For a shorter or longer time, the individual may have to submit to the modification of some rights and something very close to the disappearance of others, if Society is not to perish and all his rights with it. In war his right to life may not prevent his being put in the front line where the loss of his life may be a practical certainty: his right to property cannot prevent the State taking what it needs for the common defence; the right of association may have to be suspended for all men, when evil men may use it for the peril of Society. And there will be interference not only with these statable rights, but with the area in which men have been accustomed to exercise responsibility and freedom of choice. The Government may have to make decisions for all—as to the crops men shall grow, or the work they shall do—and take to itself what in normal times would be responsibilities exercised by the individual—but this upon the condition that the rights are abrogated only for the time of the crisis and when the crisis is over will be restored: they still exist though not in operation: the rights, in fact, are suspended for the sake of the rights.

The special difficulty today is that crisis, which used to be exceptional, has become the norm. No one can see forward to the end of crisis. We have come through two world wars, and may be about to be engulfed in a third.

But we shall be misjudging the realities of our situation, if we think that war and the possibility of war are the whole cause of the crisis in which we so obviously are. If it were so, everything would be easier. We should only have to win the war, and normal times would be here. But we have won two wars without bringing order back to our world; and if there is another war, and we win that too, we shall still not have order. Merely beating off pirates does not make the ocean peaceful or the ship seaworthy. The fact is that, war or no war, things are largely out of control. Blind forces are running wild, and no one knows what to do about them. The ambition and greed for power or money of individuals and nations are not in this sense blind, but they stir blind psychological and economic reactions. There are psychological forces surging up within man; and there are strange economic forces crashing in on us: material things have grown too big for man to handle: everything man does has strange repercussions and no one, not even Caesar, knows what they will be. In a tornado it would be ridiculous to be aiming at perfecting the details of life on shipboard. We must reduce everything to a handful of ultimate principles, perhaps two ultimate principles: obedience to the law of God and reverence for man.

At so late a stage in this book, it should not be necessary to say again that no emergency justifies an ignoring of God's laws, for they are the laws of reality, and in a conflict with reality man will always lose. Nor should it be necessary to repeat that reverence for man is the fundamental social law, so that if it goes, nothing is left. Yet one cannot feel that in our present tornado either governors or governed are very acutely conscious of either principle—certainly not of the principle of reverence. Yet in crisis reverence is more needed in the social order than in normal times. When man's rights are clearly defined and granted to him without question, it may not be so important to remember that reverence is at the base of them. The rights themselves ensure that men will be treated properly. But when so many of the rights have to be taken away, then reverence is most urgently needed. And in the particular crisis in which we now are, reverence is most difficult. In wartime, men can be brought to a high pitch of energy and sacrifice—during the air raids in England, reverence for the ordinary man was not difficult. But with the special stimulus of mortal peril withdrawn, men are not acting like heroes, or even very much like men, but rather like hypnotized rabbits, than which nothing is harder to revere.

Reverence, I say, is essential. If decisions must be made for men which they used to make for themselves, if the area of human freedom has to be diminished, Caesar should make the decisions and diminish the freedom with a full awareness of the gravity of what he is doing, and a determination to restore what he has taken from men as soon as the crisis is over. Caesar should feel like that: the citizens should feel like that. And in fact, neither feels like that. The modern bureaucrat has real compunction when he cuts the food ration, but none at all when he cuts the area of individual freedom and responsibility—because he knows that the body grows by food and he does not know that the personality grows by responsibility.

The bureaucrat being thus insensitive, the citizen should be doubly sensitive. But for the most part, we are not. We realize that something is being taken from us which we used to have, and which in our poor way we valued. There is momentary annoyance, but hardly more than momentary. We see, when the first irritation is over, that Caesar had good reason; then, unless things go very badly, we get used to the deprivation, grow comfortable in it, cease to wish the old right restored, forget that we ever had it. It is curious how little sensitive men can be to a diminishment of their essential manhood, provided they are comfortable. It is a little depressing to note how few wars there have ever been for freedom. Most wars for freedom have been wars against oppression, which is a very different matter: if the tyrant had been kind, he would not have been very much resisted. The trouble is that the tyrant never is kind, not for long anyway. If men give up freedom for the sake of some other good, they do not even get the other good in permanency; partly because with the loss of freedom they lose the vitality without which they will not keep any other good.

This want of sensitiveness to an assault upon the human personality has always been a human characteristic. But it is especially evident in our own day, for the very idea of personality has gone into eclipse.

15

Personality in Eclipse

PERSONALITY HAS two meanings, and in both it is in eclipse.

The first is the philosophical meaning, the one I have been mainly using throughout this book, which states the fact that men are beings with a spiritual element, capable of knowing and loving.

The other is personality as it figures in ordinary speech: a man is said to have a strong or weak personality, colourful or negative, or any one of twenty other adjectives, all referring to the impact that the man makes upon others.

Personality in the first sense distinguishes men from animals, vegetables and minerals; personality in the second sense distinguishes men from one another. By the first, we are men, it is of man's essence to have personality, and in having it men are alike. The second expresses each particular man, it goes with man existential, and by it all men are different: it makes for richness and a fruitful diversity of response and experience in the life of society.

The two meanings are very closely connected. There is a common error that links personality to external oddness. A young woman will be a personality because she leads a leopard on a leash down the Rue de la Paix, an old woman because, being a grandmother, she dances all night or pilots an aeroplane or swims the Channel. All this is foolishness, and pathetic. Personality is complexion, not cosmetic; it is the outward expression of an inner reality, not something stuck on from outside. The error arises from a desire for uniqueness. But in fact every person is unique, simply by being himself. And personality in the popular sense has no value save as the expression of what we are. If we want to have a more dynamic personality, we must become more dynamic persons, not simply think up more dynamic things to do. If we want to be unique, we must simply let ourselves be ourselves. The personality that we show is the expression of the personality that we are. Both should grow, and should grow together.

Man is a union of matter and spirit but, alike both in what he is and in what he does, spirit is decisive. When we speak of a man's personality, we are almost entirely concerned with what flows from his spirit: his appearance will be part of what we call his personality, but only a subsidiary part; what really makes it is what he knows, what he likes and dislikes, the quality of his judgments, the sort of decisions he makes, his choices: and all these are expressions of his spirit—his body cannot know, love, judge, decide, choose. And it is well that it should be so. Otherwise people would soon cease to be interesting. Nothing is more boring, for instance, than a beautiful face, if it is no more than that—we see it all the first time, there is no more to see the hundredth time, there are no depths to explore, no development to be expected. But in the spirit there are depths beyond depths inexhaustibly.

As the person grows, the personality grows. Just as the body has a great mass of powers which learn to function by functioning, and in functioning grow more powerful, so with the whole personality. The intellect develops thinking power and knowing power by thinking and knowing, the will develops loving power and the power of decision by loving and deciding, passions and emotions are brought into control and are stronger for the control and not weaker. The result of right use is a soul and body matured and functioning together, so that the person himself is more real, more apt for action, and the outward expression of the personality is richer and more diverse.

(1)

In both senses personality has been under attack for a long time. For a century or more we have seen the denial of personality to man; and in our own generation we have seen the flattening of personality in men. By the denial, the distinction between man and the lower animals was diminished; by the flattening the distinction between one man and another was diminished. Both movements are worth a close look.

The attack upon the very idea of personality is the most singular fact in the history of Western man. It seemed that the human person could not see personality anywhere affirmed, but must rush to deny it. The personal devil went first, and was perhaps not very much missed. It was comprehensible that man should want to cleanse the mind's landscape of a monster so terrifying. In other words, the personal devil may have been rejected not through any dislike of personality, but only of him. But the gradual wearing away of belief in a personal God is a very different matter. Only a profound disease within the human personality could have made men feel happier in a universe ruled by blind tendencies or blind forces, tendencies and forces without knowledge or love, mighty for destruction, having no kinship with the nobler elements in man himself. There may, perhaps, have been some solace for man's egoism in that, with God gone, man was now at the head of the universe, with no being superior to himself, no being entitled to his adoration or submission, no one at all to whom he must bend his knee. If it was a solace, it was a poor solace and could hardly have lived long. If there be no God, man is indeed at the top of the universe, but of a shrivelled universe, which is at once unworthy of him and in the long run too strong for him. There being no God, the universe has no meaning, and man's life in it no meaning. Man found himself at the head of a procession, which is always fun, but the procession was going nowhere, and the fun began to wear pretty thin.

The truth is that whereas man in his essence is made in God's image, he tends to remake himself in the image he has of God. Man's personality was not likely to survive God's. Nor did it. With infinite spirit denied, finite spirit was explained away, so that man was not different in kind from the animals. Then came the Darwinian theory, and man found himself actually akin to these creatures to which he was so like in kind. And one philosophy followed another. Man found that he was not free—he gathered from the Freudians he met that libido made all his decisions for him. He found that he was not particularly valuable—as an individual accidental and strictly temporary, as a race accidental and temporary too (though the time was longer), not the heir of all the ages, but the species at present insecurely dominant and certain to be superseded.

Whatever Mr. Justice Holmes, of the United States Supreme Court, meant in saying he was unable to see any real difference between a man and a baboon and a grain of sand, the average man was by then far too reduced either to feel capable of telling him what the difference might be or even to resent his inability to see one.

Yet with all this false philosophizing, leading to a total devaluation of man, some instinct kept him functioning as a man and treating others as men. There is a deep health in the human person which unhealthy ideas do not at once corrupt; we tend to be better than our worst ideas; men can act healthily while thinking falsely or confusedly; indeed what men tell themselves they think is not always what they do think. But this is a dangerous condition. Unless some instinct or good habit keeps the life of man untainted, sooner or later the false thought seeps into and transforms the depths of the mind, and men find themselves at last acting down at the level of their philosophy. That is why the more recent flattening of human personality has been so disastrous. It has meant a whole mass of maltreatments of the human person, which fit only too well with the theoretical devaluation of human personality.

When I speak of maltreatments, I am not thinking of concentration camps or forced-labour camps and lethal chambers for human beings, though these are the entirely logical outcome of the false philosophy about man. I have in mind practices which have become normal in our own countries, by which men are dealt with as masses—radio, television, digests selling in millions, book clubs choosing the reading of millions, great national advertising campaigns. In all the history of mankind there has been nothing in the least like this, and only a very profound faith in the indestructibility of the human spirit can give confidence that it will stand up to so much battering. The common element in all of them is the necessity under which they operate of ignoring the elements by which men differ and concentrating upon the elements in which men are alike. The advertiser *must* talk to all men as though they would all respond alike. As a fact, different men have different tastes in books or magazines or furniture or drinks or shaving cream or any one of a thousand things. But if these differences in taste are to be respected, then we can never have a national advertising campaign at all. So the advertiser cannot talk to the men who exist, he invents a composite man who does not exist, and persuades all men to see their own likeness in that. He needs a faceless mass, for if he dared to contemplate a variety of human faces, his slogans would die in his throat. So he talks to us as if we all had the same face, which we are beginning to have.

I have said that the differences between one man and another are a nuisance to the men who operate the mass media, and that they work upon the elements in which men are alike. And it is not the *essential* likeness that they work on, the fact that every man has an immortal spirit made in God's image, but a sort of existential likeness which they are bringing into being by a constant appeal to one set of responses and a constant ignoring of all others. They have found that they get the best results if they play upon fear—so that people wonder if other people are smelling them, and dare not look at their own toothbrush—upon covetousness—by describing their product lushly enough, they can make men drool for it—and upon envy—if the people next door have it, it is intolerable that we should be without it. And just as their propaganda ignores the fruitful differences between one man and another, and therefore tends to flatten them out of existence, so the nationally used products carry on the work. They cannot give each man what each man wants, because men are so different; so they try to give them all an approximation—not exactly what they want, but containing sufficient of what they do want to make them put up with, and ultimately come to be pleased with, the part they don't want. The whole argument is that if we all take the same standardized article, ignoring our own special requirements, we shall get it more cheaply. I am not enough of an economist to know whether this is true or not. But if it is, it means that we have settled down to getting a lot of things which are not exactly what we want instead of fewer things which are. In fact we are growing into the kind of person that wants what he's given; and we do not even notice that, with all these innumerable things to make us happy, we are not happy.

I have looked at these two companion processes—the theoretical denial and the practical flattening—only briefly. Everyone can document both abundantly from his own experience. It is no exaggeration to say that we are letting ourselves be unmanned. That disused word may be forced back into use in a new and bleak sense. When the hero of the Victorian novel said "I am unmanned," he meant that he wanted to cry: it would not have mattered very much if he had. But what is happening to us matters very much indeed. We have only to reflect upon what a man is to know that men nowadays do not see themselves as men, do not handle themselves or force others to treat them as men, but as not quite men. We still choose our sins, as men always have, but these unman us still further. And the result of it all is discouragement, from feeling that we are not anything in particular and are not going anywhere in particular; and fatigue because we have to face a universe that is bigger than we are and at the moment seems to be quite out of control, without the resources which have always strengthened man in the face of the universe. For so many of our powers are atrophied from want of exercise, and we are undernourished, because we have broken the vital contact between the reality of ourselves and the Reality that is God. Freedom and responsibility are necessities and not luxuries merely, to a healthy man; but to a fatigued and discouraged man they do not seem to be either. We have let ourselves be made into un-men, and it is hard to expect the State to treat us as men.

(2)

The State, in fact, seems rather to prefer us unmanned. In so far as this leads to a lack of civic energy, it leaves Caesar to run things unimpeded; in so far as it leads to a diminution of personal initiative, it facilitates that orderly arrangement of Society that Caesar can hardly help rejoicing in. The men who govern Society have always found man a most unsatisfactory material to work in, for reasons given in some detail in Chapters 4 and 5. To the organizing mind, man is a nightmare. Marx dreamed fond dreams of a society like an ant-heap or a beehive! Bernard Shaw wanted to abolish the British working classes and replace them with sensible people. In the appalling complexity of modern social and political and economic life, man's incalculability must seem to Caesar quite intolerable, and anything that will reduce it seems to need no further justification. The ruler feels that he is trying to solve the worst sort of jigsaw puzzle, with pieces that will not stay put. The trouble is not so much with man's body as in his spirit. The body has a few simple desires, and Caesar has learnt that if these are gorged, the man is satisfied—which might be one reason why so many totalitarian governments are encouraging sexual freedom to the very limit while reducing political freedom to nothing at all.

In the democracies, we have not gone so far. We are merely making tentative steps in the same direction. As we have already seen, it is a human tendency to think more of how a piece of work can be done best than of how it is best for man that it should be done. In Chapter 3 we draw the moral of the adding machine. From its introduction into business offices there have been two results—all the additions are correct, and everybody has lost the mental capacity to add a column of figures. It was not a great capacity, but it *was* one: one mental muscle that used to work, works no more. I used the adding machine merely as an illustration of a profoundly important social principle, that there are all sorts of things which it is better for man that he do for himself, even if they could be done better for him. Every time something is taken from man that he once did, his power of operation is diminished. He is less of a man.

The trouble is that if you consistently treat the man's good as primary, the work may be done less well; and as we have said, it is a human tendency to concentrate upon the excellence of the work, rather than the spiritual well-being of those who do it. Caesar, because he is doing so great a work, has this tendency at very high intensity. The job he is trying to do seems so massive, and individual men so minimal, that he would be more than human if he kept the real proportions in his mind. If he is really in love with his job, he will probably be so concentrated upon producing the most efficient organization of society, that any resultant cramping of the human spirit will seem to him irrelevant. But to the extent of his neglect of man, his work is condemned. The most admirable new car is not admirable at all, if the passenger cannot sit straight in it. One can imagine the manufacturer saying, "Sorry, our new streamlining techniques don't really allow for passenger comfort. But they make a better car—speedier, easier to handle in traffic, consuming less gas. And one must not worry about the passengers. In a generation or two, the human shape will have adapted itself. . . ." One *can* go mad on machinery: there is something hypnotic about it. And there is no machinery upon which men can go more totally mad than the machinery of society.

Note the key phrase—"In a generation or two, the human shape will have adapted itself." It is the dream of the modern ruler, whether he be a totalitarian autocrat, or the elected representative of a democracy. The only difference is, that the totalitarian ruler is not content to wait for a generation or two, but tries to speed up the process: his aim is to create the man who will fit the society—in fact, to produce the necessary distortions. Hitler actually said it: "I will create a violently active, intrepid, brutal youth before whom the world will shrink back." He would create! Indeed he made a very good attempt, and in the few years since his death psychology has developed further techniques for the "conditioning of men," and there are still totalitarian autocrats to use the new techniques and urge the psychologists for more. Within limits, they may succeed. It is possible to conceive a man whose intellect has been damaged to the point where it responds only to suggestions, and makes no judgments of its own, and a will so damaged that it could move to action only under compulsion, and not by any impulse from within. Such a man would be a human person only as an idiot is a human person; he would still retain the essential constituents of a person, but so crippled in action and response that he could be treated as a thing and feel no resentment, feel nothing, indeed, that he had not been conditioned to feel.

Such a being is conceivable, and it may be possible to remake a whole society on that gruesome pattern. It would, of course, be a slave society. Between the wars it was common enough to hear the Soviet tyranny talked of as an exploration of the profounder possibilities in democracy, or as the coming to birth of a new and dynamic concept of freedom. A good deal of ingenuity was displayed in the effort to show that it did not contradict freedom. But if one started at the other end, and asked what are the essentials of slavery, and which of these essentials is lacking in the Soviet system, the discussion usually tapered off. Now, indeed, with the full-scale remaking of man there envisaged, you would have a slavery more enslaving than any known: for the worst sort of slave owner might flog slaves into obedience, but he did not "condition" them out of the very possibility of disobedience. The slave, old-style, weighed the disobedience against the flogging: and if he usually (not always) chose obedience, he was still making a choice: so much of humanity remained to him. But the slave, new-style, will have lost the faculty of choice. Slavery means the total imposition of one man's will upon another: in the past it could only be upon another's actions: it will have reached the extreme, below which there are no further depths, when it is upon another's being.

Only men hypnotized by their own dream—dream of an ideal society to be created or dream of their own personalities to be imprinted upon generations of men not yet born —could envisage so sacrilegious an enterprise. It is sacrilege both against God and against men, for it is playing at God and smashing God's image in men. Like all sacrilege, it is also foolishness. It is aimed at permanence, and the one thing it cannot have is permanence. It seeks to reshape man according to the psychological fad of the moment, as though psychological fads never changed, and to meet the needs of the moment, as though another moment might not have different needs. In the practical order it would produce a type of man who had lost the marvellous adaptability of men, for which the unadaptable miracles of machinery are no substitute. In the organic order it would have ensured a breed of devitalized men, from whom no vitality could pour into the machine of society.

(3)

In our own countries, there is no present prospect of any such remaking of man to meet society's needs. Our Caesar does not deny the majesty of God or make any frontal assault upon the nature of man. But neither is his primary consideration, or seen by him as essential for the success of his own particular work. In a general way he wants to serve man, and more vaguely still he honours God, but he makes no close study either of man or of God, and would regard any such study as totally extraneous to the conduct of his State, and perhaps rather too frivolous for a man so busy as he upon such great concerns as have been entrusted to him. Certainly he does not realize that the Common Good can only be damaged by treating man as un-man or God as un-God.

The ruler no more than the doctor can serve men without studying them, which means studying the general context of the reality in which they are, and themselves within that context. Well-meaningness is not more adequate as a qualification for a ruler than for a doctor. We are back at the parable sketched in an earlier chapter about Foulon who told the hungry they could eat grass and Marie Antoinette who asked the hungry why they did not eat cake. The one was cruel, the other was kind, but both were catastrophic. Today we see other societies ruled by cruel Caesars, our own by kindly Caesars. We may thank God that we are spared the cruelty: but a moment may easily come when we may pray God to be spared the kindness. What we want is rightness, and kindness is no substitute.

As Christopher Dawson has pointed out, the kind Caesar presents a special sort of difficulty that the other does not. If Caesar comes at you with a machinegun, the intellectual problem is simple. He is evil, and should be resisted. You may not be able to resist him, or even have courage enough to try, but at least your mind is clear. But the humanitarian Caesar who comes at you with an armful of milk bottles has you in total uncertainty—especially if you have elected him yourself. He is not evil. Milk bottles are even less evil than he. Yet he may be a most insidious threat to the human personality. If his kindness involves treating men as they are not—as it almost certainly will, since he has made no study of man—then we shall be diminished by it and may even be destroyed by it.

None of this is fanciful. The signs of it are already clearly present and they are increasing. The Welfare State is noble in motive, but it invariably proceeds by providing more and more things for men which once they provided for themselves; and this involves making decisions for men which once they made for themselves, undertaking responsibilities which once were theirs, and so inevitably making them less capable of decision and choice and responsibility —and diminishing, in other words, the special qualities that distinguish man from animals and vegetables, the special qualities that make him man. So far the movement has not invaded the inner citadel of personal morality. It has affected more external things, like medical services and housing. It has begun, and indeed gone very far in, the control of education, and there is no reason to think that that particular invasion has reached its limit. Of all, it is perhaps the most dangerous to freedom.

Every tyrant has made it a first aim to get control of the schools, so that he may train the new generations in the ideas that he wishes them to hold. In such schools the children will not learn what their rights are against the State, or indeed that they have any such rights. As we have seen, education as a whole should be a function of Society as distinct from the State, the education of a given child the responsibility of his parents primarily. Only so shall we have the right order in which the citizens get the State they want as against the monstrous perversion of order in which the State gets the citizens it wants. Every tyrant, I say, has taken over the schools. Our own democracies look like doing the same thing.

And even this is not the end. We have conceded every principle which would prevent the State from making any interference in men's personal lives, if it could be presented as for the Common Good. The step from allowing birth-control and encouraging birth-control to imposing birth-control is not an unthinkably long step in the modern atmosphere. Voices, even clerical voices, have been raised against the evil of letting parents decide to go on having children, "thus giving Society more mouths to feed." The same voices have been raised in favour of sterilizing whole sections of the community. If some well-meaning lunatic urges—as Samuel Butler and Bernard Shaw urged—that it is better for children to be taken from their parents and brought up in institutions, he will find more followers now than those pioneers found. There is no mistaking the direction and intensity of the invasion, or the certainty that the flood is rising. There are two reasons.

The first is paternalism, an expression of the universal tendency to play at being God, restrained in our democracies by the desire to be a beneficent God. It is a total misconception of the State's function. You cannot make men moral by Act of Parliament, as the State knows well enough. But you cannot make them happy by Act of Parliament, either, nor indeed is that the State's job. The State should provide the conditions in which men can set about making themselves happy. Paternalism is a bad thing in a family. If it succeeds, it produces spineless children: if it fails, it produces rebellious children: and it is very bad for the father. If paternalism is a bad thing in a family, where if anywhere it belongs, it can only be a worse thing in the State.

But there is another reason, and to this we have already alluded. All life has become so complex that the job of running a modern State can be quite maddeningly so. There is the tornado of which something was said in the last chapter—the whole social, political and economic situation seeming to be out of control; and even if one may hope that in a generation or two man will have asserted some control, at best the task of government can never be easy again. It is natural, therefore, for Caesar to try to reduce the complication a little, by making more of the decisions himself and leaving fewer to the variousness and incalculability of the individual. He has the power to do it, for he controls the use of force and the means of propaganda. The citizen may feel anything from irritation to frenzy, but most of all he feels helpless. The machinery of Society is too complex. If Caesar were suddenly to say to him, "All right, *you* handle it," he would not know where to begin. The one hope is if Caesar himself will at once reverence man, and see what reverence for man involves, not only in itself, but for Caesar's own functioning: for no perfecting of the social machinery will compensate for man devitalized. Vitality, indeed, is the sociological problem—how to get it, how to preserve it.

If Caesar can master this, he will learn incidentally what things make for vitality in himself, for he too is human: but what matters from Society's point of view is that he will so act as to encourage the forces that make for life in it. Societies die when they become too tired to go on making the effort that healthy social life demands. Human vitality is of the body and of the spirit—especially of the mind as it takes hold of truth and the will as it copes with the situations that confront it. But bodies and minds belong only to individual men. The State has no body of its own and no mind of its own. Vitality, then, has its source in the human person, and any vitality the State has must come from its members. The State has even less power to make them vital than to make them moral; but it can provide the conditions for vitality and remove the obstacles, above all not *be* an obstacle. If the citizens lack vitality, the State has nowhere else to go to get it; there is no way of revitalizing the State without revitalizing the citizens. That is why Caesar must study what things make for vitality in his subjects and what things diminish it. This is no academic study, but of the utmost practicality.

Caesar, in short, must understand Society. He must know the techniques, political, sociological, economic, by which he can secure the results that he wants; otherwise, with the best moral principles, he will produce only a well-intentioned mess. But he must also know the profounder laws, as that Society exists in order that Man may be more fully Man, and that in the relations of men love is essential: as we have seen, Christ's commands to love God and our neighbour are the most practical of social rules. He must understand Society in order that he may conduct its affairs competently; he must understand it also in order that it may be not only well managed, but alive.

16

Vitality

VITALITY obviously flows from health; and a thing is healthy when it is fully itself, and functioning fully and freely as itself. Any cramping or distorting of the self makes it less healthy and therefore less vital; powers unused, needs unmet, diminish health and vitality still further.

There is a vital interchange between being and operating; any interference with either is, quickly or slowly, destructive.

(1)

It is of man's essence to be intelligent and free, capable therefore of judging and deciding; to make all the judgments and take all the decisions for him devitalizes him as certainly as if one stopped him using his arms or legs. There may be a dozen excellent reasons for keeping him from either the spiritual or the bodily operations, man's own indolence may even welcome being relieved of trouble, but nothing can prevent either sort of disuse from damaging health and lowering vitality.

All this may seem quite intolerably obvious; but our own generation has developed an extraordinary skill in muddying the obvious. So that, for example, it can be enthusiastically held that men are not being deprived of judgment and decision, so long as the ruler, who does all the judging and deciding for them, is of their own choice. But to judge that the ruler knows best, to decide to let *him* decide, while it may make the whole situation "constitutional," does not give men's judging and deciding faculty the exercise both need, if the men are to be healthy men. They are simply a judgment in favour of not judging, a decision to let the power of decision sleep.

No word or idea has suffered so much from the muddying process as Freedom. There was a time when a Liberal was a man who believed in the maximum of leaving people alone. Now he is a man who believes in the maximum of interference, for the individual's good. There have always been men who thought something else more valuable than liberty—as the Prohibitionist thinks sobriety, and the doctrinaire his system. Today's Liberal thinks comfort or security or equality more valuable than liberty, and sees nothing odd in continuing to call himself a Liberal. Provided it is for their own good that men are being managed, provided each man has some minutely fractional say in choosing the managers, the Liberal is satisfied that liberty is not violated. The muddying process is complete. The word liberty can no longer be used as the test whether a Society is well ordered. Responsibility must be the test—whether or not the whole trend of a society is towards letting men make their own judgments and decisions about the conduct of their lives.

I have used the word trend. Responsibility need not be an obsession or a shibboleth. We have seen again and again throughout this book that there are judgments and decisions that must be made by the State for the good of all. But unless there is an awareness of the value of personal responsibility for the individual, a steady tendency to preserve it, an instinctive dislike of any measure that curtails it, then it will not survive; and Society will not survive either. The mentality that would rather see England free than see England sober is essential to health: it is not a law of the Medes and Persians, but it is a wonderful state of mind. The people who would prefer England sober are prepared to curtail personal responsibility; so are the people whose dream is geometrical equality or any other sort of geometrical symmetry in social and political life.

One may write all these off as cranks, or at any rate as a minority and eccentric. But the desire, or better the passion, for social welfare, for the widest possible distribution of whatever things are seen as good, is not the fad of a handful of cranks. It is an idea noble in itself, so that there is something mean in the man who is not moved by it. And it is the dynamic idea behind the growth of the State as the great nursing mother of us all, which is the greatest present threat to personal responsibility and therefore to vitality.

People must be fed and housed and healed and taught. But why by the State? For the reason we have already seen urged in support of the great national advertising campaigns which have us all buying the same handful of products. If the State provides the same service for everybody, then we shall all get it a little cheaper. And it has exactly the same disadvantage, that we none of us get exactly what we want, but only a rough approximation to what the average man is assumed to want. When the State provides education for everybody, the parent does not get exactly the school he wants for his children, or the education he wants for them; when the State provides a universal medical service, the patient does not get the doctor he wants: what is worse, he does not get the relation with the doctor that he personally would choose to have. So that the great flattening process continues on a vaster scale than the richest advertiser could afford. From the point of view of the human being, it would be immeasurably better for the State to see to it that each man has the opportunity to earn enough to pay for medical care and his children's education, making his own arrangements with the doctor, and choosing the school that offers the sort of education he likes best.

I say it would be immeasurably better. And this is not simply a private quirk of my own. The vast majority of people would see it as better. Yet as a matter of practical politics, it is not even suggested. The reasons why it is not suggested are full of instruction for the man who would understand our present strangeness. The first is that it would cost more for each citizen to make his own choices: and in our present condition that sounds final. Which it is not. Assuming, as the taxpayer finds it difficult to assume, that the State effects a saving by handling everything, we are only back at our answer to the national advertiser. If it would cost more for an individual to get the schools and the medical service of his own personal choice, then it is still better to have a lesser amount of the things one actually wants than a larger amount of the things that are not quite, and in many instances not at all, what one wants. And we can go deeper still. It is better to be more complete as human beings than to have more time in school or more medical care. Personal responsibility is of greater value than either learning or medicaments.

The second reason is that if the whole effort of the State were directed to seeing that every man had the opportunity to earn enough to provide medical care and education for his own family, some would waste the extra money upon beer or women or horses, and their children would go unschooled and unhealed. A minority, a small minority, would act precisely so. But because some would abuse personal responsibility, to take personal responsibility from all is a horrible shortsightedness. And it is growing as a governmental principle. Because some cannot be trusted, a machinery is set up which treats all as untrustworthy, so that trust vanishes from the relation of the citizens with the State. A healthy Society would find some way of dealing with the irresponsible and untrustworthy minority, while preserving responsibility and trust as the norm of life. President Roosevelt is said to have explained his policy (in relation to Stalin, as it happens) by saying, "The way to make an untrustworthy man trustworthy is to trust him." Perhaps he never said it. But somebody said it: I did not invent it. It is quite farcically untrue. But the reverse is painfully close to the truth: the way to make a trustworthy man untrustworthy is to mistrust him. Once the State puts in an inspector, it becomes a matter of course, almost a point of honour, to trick him: certainly there is no public opinion against your doing so. The State says we're untrustworthy: very well, let us be. So the State must put on more inspectors. For the State, as for the individual, it is better to be occasionally deceived than permanently suspicious.

Why do the mass of people not see personal responsibility and initiative, the power to judge and decide, as essential to manhood, as things, therefore, which must be regarded as primary: so that the first object of the social order is their preservation, so that they shall not be, as they now are, allowed to exist as best they can when all sorts of other requirements have been met? Because the State which existed before the advent of the Welfare State had as little care for these human values in the majority of citizens as the Welfare State in all. The minority who ruled, whether they were an aristocracy or merely rich, valued personal initiative tremendously for themselves. But for a long time they kept it to themselves. The majority were not allowed to use it any more then than now. They had no habit of it and no instinct to fight for it. The man who would start a campaign for it now finds no nerve in the majority of men thrilling to life in response. Even those who concede that theoretically he may be right, and that a restoration of personal responsibility would in itself be a good thing, would hold that it is not practical and that one wastes one's time by bothering about it at all. But it is never a waste of time to be thinking about the ideal. We should, indeed, give a great deal of thought to what we want; to be thinking exclusively of what we can get is limiting and dingy. Merely wanting is already one condition for getting; things come closer into the realm of the possible simply by being desired. And this is something we had better desire. There is no vitality without it.

(2)

Health is there when Man is being himself and functioning fully and freely as himself—when, in fact, Man Existential is in the fullest harmony with Man Essential. We have just been considering Man as a spiritual being capable of judgment and decision, and the danger to health that comes from any cramping or distortion of these powers. But there are other elements which go to Man's essence so that their free functioning is a condition of health. Two of these—that Man is a social being, and that Man does not belong to this world only—must also be considered. Let us consider first Man as a social being.

There is no point in repeating here all that has already been said about Society as rooted in the nature of Man. There is the human tendency to reach out towards other men—the tendency which makes solitary confinement so great a horror; and the plain fact that men gain from contact and collaboration, and are incapable of reaching their full stature without them. The collaboration can be on the smallest scale and the largest, there are human powers that find an outlet and human needs that find a satisfaction in every sort and at every level of collaboration. It is a mistake to think that operations too large for individuals or families should as a matter of course be taken over by the State. It is an actual impoverishment of Man if he is not allowed to develop his powers of working with large bodies of his fellows *at his choice*. Schools, hospitals, industrial enterprises that are far beyond the powers of individuals or families can well be carried on by groups less than the State, and it is good that they should be. It is always better for Man, other things being equal, that the sphere of choice should be as large as possible and the sphere of compulsion as small. Voluntary co-operation with others is valuable simply *as* voluntary, for the power it gives men for the exercise of personal responsibility in the choice of objectives and means and associates; and it is the best preparation for the obligatory co-operation that life in the State demands. The State, if it is wise, will cherish it.

Of all human groupings less than the State, the Family is the one that matters most, and the destruction or cramping of whose functions is most devitalizing. It is naturally superior to the State, prior to it in origin, and closer to the very roots of human vitality. It is the Society in which Man is most fully himself, seen as himself, valued as himself. A family does not tend to think of the Father as a member of the middle class, or as a plumber, or as a unit of personnel, but as the particular person that he is.

The family everywhere is under tremendous pressures, not unlike those we have seen brought to bear upon the individual personality. There is a similar theoretical devaluation and a similar flattening in fact. Of the latter—the economic changes, which have made the family practically cease to be an economic unit, the social changes (in entertainment, for example) which have made the home little more than a place to sleep in—it is impossible to say anything that everyone does not know. But it is worth while to consider the theoretical attack. The family, like the individual man, has always been difficult for the planners to fit into their ideal social orders. It involves an element dynamic, three-dimensional, with an incalculability that seems to raise ordinary human incalulability to a higher power. It is as much the nightmare of the planners as Man himself. Their whole instinct is to ignore it and ultimately to abolish it. Plato saw no function for it in his ideal Republic, and most subsequent designers of ideal societies have been no more friendly to it.

In the one Utopia that was meant to be brought into

existence—Karl Marx's Classless Society—it has no place at all. It has been most instructive to watch the ups and downs of the Soviet effort to live up to the Master's ideas on the family. There was, to begin with, a vast effort to destroy it: divorce was made easier than in any other great community (with the explanation added that no sensible proletarian would be guilty of a weakness so bourgeois as jealousy); children were taken from their mothers practically at birth, thus in one act freeing children from their families and freeing mothers for the factories; fathers lost the right to discipline those equal fellow-citizens, their small sons. But it did not work. It was found that the proletarian was as liable to jealousy as any bourgeois and even more liable to kill for it; that mothers were disinclined for the anguish and labour of having children if, at the end of it, they were not allowed to keep them; that if fathers might not discipline their children, the State found a torrent of delinquency on its hands that it could not begin to cope with. The result was that Russia set about a grand-scale restoration of family life; but their frantic dream of some day abolishing it, and thus leaving no social group between the individual and the collective, is still with them. And there are new techniques that promise better success next time: as against the unwillingness of mothers to bear children save on their own terms, there is now the test-tube; as against juvenile delinquency, there are possibilities of institutions and psychological conditioning.

But it is not only where the Marxist dream is in process of realization that the family is under attack. Progressive thinkers everywhere are pointing out happily that its usefulness is vanishing rapidly. Its economic functions are going—the family no longer works or produces as a unit;

and while the father still does in general support his wife and children, the end of this is just over the horizon, with the State educating the children, providing doctors for the whole family, already beginning to provide meals and houses: so that the day does not seem necessarily far distant when we shall all be one undifferentiated mass, all citizens together, all suckled by the State.

But there is one function which, from Plato onwards, they have all, as it seems incredibly, overlooked. They have listed all sorts of lesser functions of the family and shown how these could be performed equally well without it. But the supreme function has not been mentioned at all, and for this there is no substitute. The family must do it, or it will not be done. Sociologically, the family is the one school of love; and love is the principle of life, individual life, social life.

That notably unloving men like Bernard Shaw and his master Samuel Butler did not see this, is not surprising; but that the ordinary human being should be bluffed into not seeing it is very surprising indeed. Because he has always known it, and his proverbs show that he has. All the world loves a lover, he has said down the centuries; and it's love that makes the world go round. Love—the act of loving and the certainty of being loved—has a wonderfully vitalizing effect. And this at every level, from passionate love down to comradeship—at every level, provided there is warmth and drive and some emotional quality in it. It releases energies and creates energies. It makes life worth living, and any amount of well-being shades down to a deadly gray without it. This is so obviously true of the individual, that it hardly seems worth labouring. But it is true of society too. St. Augustine's definition of society as a multitude of men united by agreement about the things they love remains the only vital definition. And for perfect health in society one of the things they must agree in loving is one another. That is what makes Christ's second command, that we love our neighbour as ourself, the only practical working rule. If Caesar does not know it, then he cannot conduct the life of the State successfully. Usually he does know it, but vaguely and with no knowledge how difficult it is to bring about.

The family is the school of love because by its very nature, unless that nature has been spoiled, it meets these two conditions. It is a group of people united by agreement about the things they love; in it people love one another as they love themselves—indeed this is the one place in which quite ordinary people love others more than they love themselves; between husbands and wives, between parents and children there is normally a readiness for sacrifice nowhere else found. Within the family, painlessly so to speak, people learn the ways of love, unselfishness, sacrifice, trust, upon the existence of which the whole of society depends. A given family, even great numbers of families, may fail in love and thus not perform this function. If they do, then for those people the function is not performed, and Society is the loser.

It is a superficial objection that intense love within the family works against a general love of the community and of mankind as a whole. Love is the act of a loving person. Whatever tends to make a person love at all, increases his loving power. It is, as we noted in discussing Patriotism, a law of our nature that love is most intense at the centre, in relation to those closest to us, and diminishes in intensity as it moves outward. But the stronger it is at the centre, the more of it there is to radiate. The less intense at the centre, the less in the diminished fringes. It is rather like fire. It warms most those closest to it, and least those furthest from it: but you do not increase the warmth of those furthest by damping it down at the centre. The people who are by way of loving all men equally, seldom love anyone much—all men are too diffused an object to concentrate will and emotions upon. The saints are a perfect example of how far the warmth of a fire can reach when it is at furnace heat at the centre. They love God so enormously that they are practically nothing but love, and there is no creature that does not feel the heat of it; yet even at that they will love some more than others, as Christ loved St. John above the other apostles. Loving someone intensely does not make one love others less. On the contrary, as we have seen, by increasing one's loving power, it makes one love them more. All the world loves a lover, and rightly. A lover loves all the world.

(3)

Vitality, that happy by-product of health, flows from man being what he is, and functioning fully and freely as what he is. We have glanced at this principle in its application to man as a union of matter and spirit, and to man as a social being. It remains to see how it bears on man as a religious being. For man is not of time only or of the finite; his life is flowing into him from the Infinite, his nature is in the likeness of the Infinite, his destiny is to come to total union with the Infinite. In discussing sociology you cannot simply take the part of man that concerns you as sociologists, and ignore the rest as though it did not exist. The religious element in man's nature is not isolated, but interwoven, interpenetrant. It may be annoying to the ruler, especially of a modern religiously neutral State, to have to take note of it. But he must all the same. That men are going from him can hardly have escaped his notice—every hour of every day subjects of his are putting themselves beyond the reach of his malice or benevolence: he should know that they are going on to another life. But he should know more than that. If he does not see that these men are made in the image of God, he will have no ground for the first qualification a ruler needs—reverence for his subjects; so much of his time he sees men at their worst, contempt for men is the abiding temptation of rulers; his experience of Man Existential, man as he meets him, must be checked and balanced by a sure vision of Man Essential, man as he profoundly is. And he will fail in the second qualification, too, realism: he will be handling men without knowing what they are, knowing only what they look like: he will be working in material he does not understand.

Quite apart from the *joy* of knowing one's material (especially if one's self be of the same material), there is the *necessity,* at the lowest utilitarian level, of knowing it. Among other things it will explain many phenomena otherwise inexplicable, which all good realists ignore, but which are in fact very bothering. A number of these were considered in the first section. Here I shall treat only of one, which concerns the ruler vitally—the extreme difficulty of making people happy, and the sheer impossibility of keeping them happy. Men find nothing too much trouble if the purpose is worth while; but life itself becomes too much trouble when no purpose is seen. The sense that life is worth living and effort worth making—that is vitality. No amount of well-being is a substitute. A stud farm is different because beasts are not made in God's image: whatever they are capable of having they can have here. But for man it is not so. The question, Is life worth living? is asked more often by the prosperous. In whatever circumstances, life, with its routine of dailiness, is a heavy strain on vitality and involves a heavy wastage of vitality.

Suffering, which no one can wholly avoid, and death, which no one can avoid at all, increase the strain and wastage. Men need to know what life is for and how suffering may be used and what death leads to. If they do not get an answer upon life and death, the mere meaninglessness of everything eats into their vital energies. If they do not get an answer upon suffering, they will either set their teeth and live through it, which may produce strength of character but as often as not issues in hardness and sullenness, and in the long run apathy, or they will collapse in self-pity or scream in hysteria. As Christopher Dawson notes in *Religion in the Modern State:* "It is the horror of this empty and sterile world, far more than any economic hardship or political injustice, that is driving men to revolutionary action." We need to be given a clear vision of human life, its origin and direction and goal, what in fact it signifies, with suffering and death seen in their place and function—suffering as usable for increase of life, death as gateway to fulness of life.

But the true vision of reality, though indispensable, is not enough. It shows life as worth living. But the efforts and resistances life calls for, still remain, are if anything increased as the horizon widens: selfhood can be a weary business. There is a burden to be borne, and we shall not bear it with no vital resources but our own. Just as the mind must be illumined by meaning, so the will must be strengthened by a new inpouring of vitality.

As against all this Caesar must recognize the limitation of his own powers to help us. Of himself, he knows no more than we do about the ultimates, and is as much in need as we are of revitalization. One way or another, we must get them from God. Caesar then must see why God is essential in Society as in marriage and should not be jealous of God any more than a husband or wife should. It is the natural tendency of the State to want to possess the whole man, as a husband and wife may want to possess each other. We find this even in democracies. There are men who work themselves into a frenzy because their fellow-citizens get their views of what comes after death, and of what therefore life means, from outside the State. But upon these matters, the State has no information of its own to give. Caesar himself needs God as much as any of his subjects, perhaps more than any of his subjects: rulers are more subject to world-weariness than the rest of us. The State, like the husband, cannot *be* God: cannot meet all man's needs, make man happy. The secular view of life can organize, but cannot vitalize.

Religion, then, is essential to Society's vitality. The trouble, from Caesar's point of view, is that religion comes to the citizens through religions, with men for officials. He may feel that he could get along with God, but God's ministers are a different proposition. The surface pattern is not the same from place to place. In one State, the citizens practically all belong to one Church; in another they are fairly equally divided between two; in a third there are a dozen or more large religious bodies: even where there is but one main Church, there are usually a number of smaller sects: in Britain and America the religious bodies run into hundreds.

Theoretically States and Churches are operating in different fields and should not conflict. As Leo XIII, speaking for the Catholic Church, points out in the Encyclical *Sapientiae Christianae:* "Church and State both possess sovereignty . . . neither obeys the other *within the limits to which each is restricted by its constitution.*" And one imagines that most Churches would say the same. But in practice conflict is pretty certain. For both have the same subjects—the people, who as citizens belong to this or that State, as men with immortal souls belong to this or that Church. Teachings, especially moral teachings, given by one Church or another may cut across Caesar's view of how the State should be run; policies initiated by Caesar in a sincere desire to do his best for Society may seem to this or that Church a contradiction of God's law or man's spiritual nature.

As we have seen in the matter of the State and the Individual, it is not always possible to draw clear lines of demarcation where one set of rights ends and another begins: human life is not geometry. Apart from that, there is the tendency power has to spread, whether it is the power of statesmen or churchmen. One remembers Henry II and Thomas à Becket, with the Archbishop confronting the royal power, and the King's knights murdering him. One remembers Cyril Lukaris, Greek Patriarch of Constantinople—not confronting the Sultan, for that would have been too risky—but subtly getting his own way on point after point, till the Sultan suddenly lost patience and had him strangled. Many a secular ruler's thoughts must have strayed longingly to Henry II and the Sultan. There is an uncertain frontier region between the spiritual and the temporal, and where there is a frontier there are bound to be incidents. But of course it need not be a matter of the sword or the bow-string. Leo XIII faces the problem in the Encyclical *Immortale Dei* and shows how with both parties realizing their own limits the worst troubles can be avoided, and for the rest, "There are occasions when another method of concord is available, for the sake of peace and liberty—rulers of the State and the Roman Pontiff come to an understanding upon special matters." Where complete satisfaction all round cannot be had, life must still go on. Religion knows that Society is necessary for man: Caesar, if he knows his job, knows that Society would lead an impoverished life without Religion. Caesar, unfortunately, does not always know his job. Where there is a serious break it is more often caused by him, for the Church always knows the God-given function of Society in human life (it is not religious men who are everywhere playing the traitor now, nor has that ever been their way), whereas secular rulers too often see the Church as a mere extra. Certainly it may very well happen that immediate problems are solved for Caesar if he gets rid of the Church or the Churches. But he is paying too high for present relief. As I hold, the Catholic Church was founded by Christ, and in it men can get the fulness of truth and life and union with God. But in every Church where God is loved, its members get something which they profoundly need and cannot get anywhere else—not from the Catholic Church because they do not believe in it and assent cannot be forced, not from the State because what they need the State has not. Without religion, the level of social vitality must fall.

(4)

One of the follies to which Caesar is liable is to prefer subjects docile and manageable—so that he reigns unquestioned, not realizing that he is the unquestioned king of the half-dead, and shapes the social and political order as he wishes, not realizing that that can never be done with a living thing.

The really competent Caesar prefers to have vital subjects, as the good rider prefers a spirited horse. There are riders, myself among them, who like their horses lifeless, and are happiest of all, indeed, on a rocking-horse. But you do not get anywhere on a rocking-horse, you only get a comfortable ride. That Caesar should be a vital and vigorous personality has always been realized. But that his subjects should in their own way be vital, as he in his, is not always so clearly grasped. There is a proverb to the effect that an army of sheep led by a lion would defeat an army of lions led by a sheep, and one sees the point. But what is really wanted is an army of lions led by a lion. Certainly a lion would be happiest leading lions; if he would rather lead sheep, he is no lion but only a sheep with delusions of grandeur. The trouble, with so many governments, is that they are by preference anonymous rulers of faceless masses.

Vitality in the governed makes problems for the governors. It is a dynamic, sometimes violent thing, and of necessity it makes for a certain unruliness—unruliness in the sense of independence and resentment at being regimented, but also in the mere variety and incalculability which makes neat arrangement impossible. There will be times when the ruler finds it maddening that men should be so, but if he knows his job and loves his job (both conditions being essential to his doing his job well) he does not really wish it otherwise. He knows that if you mechanize men, make machines of them, a large part of their unruliness disappears. And their value with it. The good ruler, working upon men, is like the good sculptor working upon stone. The sculptor sometimes curses the stone for its hardness and un-cooperativeness: dough would be so much easier—he wouldn't even need a chisel. But the resultant statue would not be worth having. There is something that stone gives to a statue that dough cannot give; and there is something that men give to the State that machines cannot give. And there is a joy and an exaltation in working in stone and in men, that a man cannot find in working in dough or machines. But the joy and the exaltation and the ultimate success all depend alike upon loving and reverencing the material one is working in.

Caesar cannot be much blamed if he sometimes wearies of men and longs for machines, as the sculptor for dough or the rider for a rocking-horse. But there is only disaster in the attempt to realize the dream. The supreme example of the machine-dough-rocking-horse mentality is the totalitarian effort to create a new man more suited to the rulers' desires. Hitler wanted and Stalin wants to create a new humanity. Christ came into the world to make a new humanity. There is all the difference between the two. For Christ, being God, is man's creator, and therefore knows man in his most intimate essence; Christ's aim was to perfect man's nature and elevate it, bringing a new principle of life into it and not damaging the life principle already there; and his way of action is to solicit man, neither coercing nor conditioning him, but respecting man's nature in the very process of healing it. In that he is the model of all who must handle men. They cannot know man as Christ knew him, but they must be ever studying man and growing in knowledge of him; and their effort must always be to find the best in man and co-operate with that. Reverence is the essential thing.

One remembers W. S. Gilbert's high official who

> Clearly knew
> The deference due
> To a man of pedigree

If only Caesar clearly knew the deference due to a man. If only we all knew it.

Index